Publish
It
Yourself

*Five Easy Steps to Getting
Your Book in Print*

Alton Pryor

Stagecoach Publishing
5360 Campcreek Loop
Roseville, CA. 95747

Publish
It
Yourself

Five Easy Steps to Getting
Your Book in Print

By Alton Pryor

ISBN 0-9660053-5-X
First Printing 2002

Library of Congress Control Number: 2002093094

Stagecoach Publishing
5360 Campcreek Loop
Roseville, CA. 95747

This book is dedicated to my son Scott, who not only designed the beautiful cover, but has guided me through all the miseries as well as thrills of coping with the intricacies of a computer.

Books by Alton Pryor

Little Known Tales in California History

Classic Tales in California History

Outlaws and Gunslingers

Those Wild and Lusty Gold Camps

California's Hidden Gold

Historic California

Jonathan's Red Apple Tree

Publish It Yourself

Table of Contents

Step 3: Printing Your Book

Step 4: Marketing Your Book

Step 5: Loose Ends

Introduction

Don't just say, "I'm going to write a book." Do it! Start today! Let me assure you, it's not impossible and it's a lot easier to self-publish a book than most would-be authors think. This manual does not intend to deal with the writing aspect of developing a book. It is assumed if you have a good topic, and know basic English grammar, you can write a manuscript, whether you use longhand, your trusty Smith-Corona typewriter, or a computer. The trouble for most new book authors comes when it's time to get a finished manuscript into book form for the world to see.

When I wrote my first book, "Little Known Tales in California History," I knew nothing about the publishing end of the newspaper, magazine and book trade. While I had been a reporter and field editor for a major magazine, I had simply written my material and submitted it to an editorial desk in a distant office. In later years, I transmitted my finished articles by modem over a telephone line.

When I finished my first 200-page book manuscript, I didn't know the next step to take. I remember saying to my wife, "Well, I have a finished manuscript, now what the hell do I do with it?"

A little research told me that publishing a book wasn't all that difficult, if one only knew what steps to follow. Yes, I made mistakes along the way, a few that were more costly than I like to think about. But by inching along, the process became clearer.

In this book, my intention is to clear the way for those who imagine that self-publishing a book is a monumental, if not impossible, task. It isn't. If you can write, you can certainly self-publish your own book. The key words are: Get Started!

Step 1

Getting Started

Why Self-Publish?

Publisher's Weekly says 7,000 new publishers come into being every year. A conservative estimate is that at any one time 50,000 small independent publishers operate across the country. These figures in themselves indicate that if others can do it, you can do it, too!

Perhaps the simplest and best answer to the question, "Why Self-Publish?" is that you will make more money doing so. Even if a major publisher, such as Random House or whomever decides that your book has enough merit for the firm to publish it, your royalties will amount to a mere 5 to 10 percent of the retail price of the book.

If a major publishing firm were to accept your book for publication, the work of marketing it would still fall on your shoulders. Unless yours is a blockbuster, you could expect little publisher support in the form of hard dollars for advertising and promotion.

Since you have to do all the grunt work yourself anyway, why not enjoy the profits. It is hard work, but it is necessary work, and you can be a success with your book. Self-Publishing is extremely satisfying work. And, it can be profitable, as thousands of self-publishers across the U.S. have demonstrated.

R.R. Bowker Company, the same firm from which you will get your ISBN (International Standard Book Number), estimates there are 1,200 new publishers coming into the marketplace every quarter. That means there are nearly 5,000 new publishers opening for business each year.

While many are failures, yours needn't be. Be aware, however, that the statistics for success are against you. According to the Midwest Book Review, there are 665,000 books currently in print, and of the 53,000 more that are published each year, only about three out of ten are financially successful.

Those who failed didn't do the necessary work to make their book a success. That is where we believe "Publish It Yourself" will help.

You could be a self-publisher by simply photocopying a booklet on a local history, stapling it together, and selling it through local shops. Your book might not be a big success, but you would still be a publisher. Self-publishing a book is doing much the same thing, but on a larger scale, where you farm the job out to printers with the proper equipment.

The Value of Self-Publishing

Estimates indicate that more than half of all books will be self-published or published by smaller presses in the next ten years. Your self-published book can sit on the shelf next to one published by one of the majors and look just as professional as theirs, without the huge costs involved.

Twin Worlds, Inc.

By self-publishing, you will see your book in print weeks or months ahead of the time it takes a large publishing house to accomplish the same task. The schedule of major publishing houses is generally on an 18-months cycle. Your schedule can be just a few weeks from the time you submit your manuscript to a printer until he returns it in the form of a finished book.

You'll find the process easy and the three or four-week wait until you receive the finished perfect-bound book an eternity. But when that delivery truck arrives, it's like Christmas coming early. You'll find the packing and shipping of books that you have been able to sell to friends and family in the interim a joy, not a job.

You'll also like making those frequent trips to the mailbox to see if there is a new order, or even better, a new check in the mail.

Richard Marek, once editorial director for Kirkus Review, as well as an editor at Macmillan and World Publishing, Dial Press, and other publishing enterprises, doesn't like the path that the big publishers are now taking.

These publishers, Marek said in a speech at an independent publishers meeting, are no longer interested in books that do not have a potential sale of 25,000 copies. These large publishing houses all want the big "killer" book and bedamned to the less commercial but worthwhile books.

He said he believed that publishing's real future lies with independent publishers who maintain control over all aspects of the publishing process.

Marek noted that the giant publishers advertise only selected titles, and the "small" books at large publishers get no advertising money at all.

Another author, Trevor Lockwood, steadfastly states, "The publishing industry has grown too big for its boots. It is time that authors, those lonely, caring souls who struggle to bring structure and meaning to a motley collection of words, were given proper recognition. Without authors, there would be no publishers, there would be no booksellers."

The self-publisher, such as yourself, has a huge advantage over the giant publishers in that you can afford to stick with a book, giving it every opportunity to find an audience. Large publishers will give up on a book almost immediately if its advance sales are small or if there are a lot of quick book returns from the bookstores.

While it may sound selfish, because it is, I personally like the trend toward self-publishing. I'm a dyed in the wool believer in self-publishing. Even though I'm writing an elementary treatise on the subject with this book, I, along with you, still have a great deal to learn. But if we learn it correctly, we will most assuredly be better off publishing our own works.

If you need an additional reason to self-publish, it might be this. You won't have to face receiving enough rejection slips from those big-house publishers to paper an office wall. With self-publishing you are strictly the boss, hopefully, a very successful and strict one.

With that in mind, let's explore our lesson plan further.

Self-Publishing Goes Back a Long Way

Huckleberry Finn, Bartlett's Familiar Quotations, The One-Minute Manager and Lady Chatterley's Lover were all originally self-published books. A good book is a good book regardless of the publisher!
R.R. Bowker

Will Your Book Sell?

"Find a 'hole' and fill it" is an old sales rep adage. It also applies to your book. If it's of interest to the general public, it will sell. If it fills a niche in a specialty group, it will sell. Just fill the niche!

A Word of Caution

Let us issue a word of caution to anyone contemplating the use of a "Vanity" or "Subsidy" publisher. Run—don't walk—away from the "Vanity" or "Subsidy" press. Under most arrangements with "Vanity" or "Subsidy" publishers, the author will provide all the upfront money.

When you self-publish, you are getting your manuscript into publishable shape, that is, making it camera-ready for the printer. A Vanity press is essentially selling you a package to do the same thing, and in return, will give the author a few copies of the book. The author will be promised royalties on any copies that the "vanity" or "subsidy" press sells. Don't hold your breath while waiting for a check.

The author could end up being out of pocket anywhere from $10,000 to $20,000 or even $30,000, and still not have any appreciable book sales. While vanity publishers may claim they will furnish all the regular publishing services, including promotion and distribution, the statistics don't back up such promises.

According to *Writer's Digest,* books published by Vanity Publishers rarely return one-quarter of the author's investment.

> *It's the ninety-nine percent of the Vanity presses that give the rest a bad name.*

Surprisingly, there are many writers who are not as anxious to make money with their book as they are in gaining a certain amount of immortality that writing and publishing a book brings.

If that is the case, and you have money to burn, the Vanity or Subsidy press route may be best for you. You'll see your book in print; although it will probably be at a considerably higher cost than if you self-publish.

By self-publishing, the author is simply bypassing all the middlemen from start to finish. The self-publisher may have to foot the bills in the process, but at least it is the self-publisher that will reap the rewards.

Now that you've made the firm decision to self-publish, lets get on with the process!

Formatting the manuscript for the printer

Many authors of how-to books on self-publishing are so intent on providing the reader with every aspect of the writing, printing, publishing and marketing processes that it is hard to wade through the choppy literary surf.

Unfortunately, some pad their text to allow them to also "pad" the retail price they charge for the book, simply because the book is thicker. That doesn't mean that books, such as "The Self-Publishing Manual," by Dan Poynter, and the "Complete Guide to Self-Publishing," by Tom and Marilyn Ross are not worthwhile; they helped guide me in publishing my first book. The author owns and enjoys several of them. You will find a number of them listed as resource material in the back of this book should you want to learn the complete ins-and-outs of the publishing industry.

With this book, the author has attempted to eliminate as much extraneous material as possible and still provide the necessary elements of getting a book into print.

The purpose of this book is to tell the reader what he needs to know and let him get on with the simple process of publishing his own book.

Publishing, or self-publishing, doesn't require the publisher to have a printing press and a shop full of equipment. These processes are jobbed out in an orderly process.

There was a time when typesetting costs made up the major portion of a book project. A self-publisher would, as little as ten years ago, have expected to pay somewhere from $6 to $10 to print and proofread each page of a 6 x 9 book. The self-publisher in those days would likely have $5000 or more invested in his or her book even before it had been sent to the printer.

Because of the computer age, new authors and self-publishers virtually eliminate the typesetting costs if they can operate a computer with a good word processing program. Of course, typesetting (computer formatting) may still be an expense if the author/self-publisher must pay to have his manuscript retyped on a computer, but the cost will be considerably less than the linotype operator of old.

The file format most requested by book printers today is called Adobe PDF format. The term, PDF, stands for *Portable Document Format.* Don't let this frighten you if you are a new computer user or some interested in self-publishing. It's not that difficult to convert your Microsoft Word file into a PDF format.

If you don't know how, take a disk copy of your manuscript to any Kinko's or Graphics firm and have them convert it. Make sure you have them embed the fonts you are using in your manuscript.

PDF files are much smaller than word processing files. Also, they can be sent as email attachments with greater ease.

Setting Up

In this book, we assume you're writing on a computer. Computers, today, are an absolute essential for most writers. Today's word processors not only provide spell checking and thesaurus programs, but correct for grammar and generally help make your words more readable.

When your manuscript is completed, a good word processing program will aid in the creation of a Table of Contents and an Index. Footnotes can also be generated. As these tasks fall more in the category of writing than they do in publishing, they will not be dealt with in great detail in this book.

Let's get started on your book. From the very beginning, I prefer writing on the same page size and font type that I will use for the finished book.

This allows me, the author, to constantly know where I am in the writing process. It allows me to know exactly how many pages I've written, even though later editing may move these pages around or even eliminate some of them. But best of all, I get a certain feel for how the book will look in print.

Keep your writing as simple as you can while still conveying your thoughts. If you're unsure that what you've said will not be understood, use my time-tested method:

Read what you've written out loud!

If it doesn't sound right when you read it out loud, you can bet your booties that it won't sound right when its read from the written page.

This book, however, is not intended as a tutoring guide in writing. It is intended solely as a guiding process to get a finished manuscript into published form. With that said, let's publish!

Type Faces and Font Sizes

By typing your manuscript in the same font size and typeface in which your book will be printed, you will quickly learn just how "readable" it is to the human eye and to your prospective customer.

When you look at the various font types, one thing should stand out: text in a serif typeface is easier to read than a sans serif face. Look at the difference:

(Serif)   **(Sans serif)**

The readers' eyes would certainly tire after staring at lengthy text in this Sans serif typeface for very long.

This doesn't mean that "sans serif" typefaces have no place in your published book. Sans serif typefaces are quite often used for headlines, tables, and similar functions.

Fonts, such as "Garamond," "Courier New", "Times New Roman" and Century Schoolbook are widely used in book printing. It boils down to a matter of personal preference. Set them up on your word processor as I've done in the following example and experiment.

This is Century Schoolbook.
This is Times New Roman
This is Garamond
This is Courier New

Of course, you're not limited to the fonts that I have listed above. Conduct your experiment with as many different typefaces as you like.

My personal preference for book text is Century Schoolbook. It is easy to read, even for people whose eyesight is becoming impaired with age. The book you are now reading is written in Century Schoolbook.

As a side note, Century Schoolbook will add a few pages to your book. Look at the examples above and you can see that Century Schoolbook is considerably expanded beyond the other typefaces, even in the short examples given.

Four factors affect the legibility of the type used. They are:

1. *Font type,* whether it is serif or sans serif;
2. *Type size,* which determines how readable it is;
3. *Leading,* (pronounced *"ledding"* which is the amount of space between the lines; and
4. *Column width.*

The human eye has been trained to read newspaper columns, and consequently, narrower columns tend to be easier to read than wide expanses of type.

If you are still uncertain after experimenting a bit with the various fonts on your word processor, consult with your printer. That's one reason you're paying him. If he is a reputable printer, he wants your finished book to look the best it can as much as you do.

With the word processing programs available on computers today, it's a simple matter to change the font or type size of an entire book without going through a major re-writing process.

Browsing books in a library or bookstore is a good way to select a typeface and to gain ideas as to how the layout of your book should look. When you see a book you really like, buy it and use it as your model. In doing so, you'll be doing another starving author a favor.

Today, virtually all books are written on a computer. Even authors that write by hand or use their old "Smith-Corona" typewriters will eventually have to have their hand-written or double-spaced, typewritten manuscript transferred onto a computer word processing program. This is the media nearly all book manufacturers use.

Today's author will almost always send the printer or book manufacturer a computer disk containing his or her book. E-mailing is now a common method of transmitting manuscripts to book printers. While many printers and book manufacturers may request a "hard copy" (printed version) of the manuscript in addition to the disk, most will work from a computer disk.

A new author, who has not yet tackled the computer world, will benefit enormously by "biting the bullet" and buying or renting a computer with a good word processing program.

Profits

There really is not a way to anticipate profits in a self-publishing venture. You may hit upon a run-away best seller, but your goal should be to break even on expenses with some profit for your time and effort in writing the book.   *R.R. Bowker*

Making the Manuscript Camera Ready

One advantage of writing and printing your book on a good word processing program is that the finished product is essentially made "camera ready" for the printer. You simply send a computer disk with the finished manuscript on it, or, email the entire book to the printer.

I have used email to send at least three of my books to a "Print On Demand" printer. The Print On Demand concept will be discussed later.

Consider the savings you gain from using a computer if you have to pay someone $4 to $10 per page to typeset your manuscript.

I personally prefer "Microsoft Word", which is the predominant word-processing software that comes on most new computers. There are others that do just as fine a job, such as Word Perfect, PageMaker, QuarkXpress and Ventura Publisher. The latter three are relatively expensive and harder to learn.

Let's assume you've gotten a computer and want to type in your manuscript, or simply change the page setup on the copy that is already on the computer. Once you determine what the "trim size" of your book will be, you need to tell the word processing program.

Book 'Trim' Sizes

There are three basic trim sizes. 4 1/4 x 6 3/4-inches, a size used most for the so-called "trade books" found on supermarket book shelves; 5 1/2 x 8 1/2-inches, which is the conventional size used for both hardcover and softcover books; and 6 x 9 inches, used more often when the book lengthy.

For our purposes, we will use a 5 1/2 by 8 1/2 inch format. This size is suitable for both hardcover and softcover, and is the most economical to print. (This book you are now reading is printed in a 5 1/2 by 8 1/2 inch format.)

For the beginning computer user, there are many classes on word processing given at community colleges and community centers at low cost. In only one or two classes you could learn the basics of word processing.

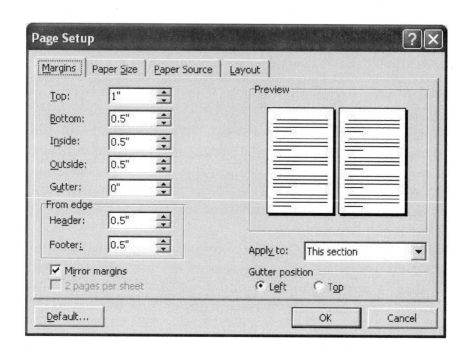

If you are using Microsoft Word as your word processor, go to *File\Page Setup* and set the margins as you see them in the page setup illustration above. Once you make the move to a computer, it isn't likely you'll return to your manual typewriter again.

Margins are used to compensate for the trimming of the book to its finished size. For this book, we have used the following margins: Top: one inch; Bottom: one-half (.5) inches; Left: .5 inches; and Right: .5 inches. Be sure to check the box *Mirror margins* on the bottom left of the screen.

The following table provides a good rule of thumb for setting book margins. You can vary them somewhat without changing the finished look of your book very much.

Typical Margin Settings

Size In inches	Margins				Final Text Area	
	Left	Right	Top	Bottom	Width	Height
4 1/4 x 6 3/4	.5	.5	.83	.5	3.25	5.5
5 1/2 x 8 1/2	.5	.5	.83	.5	4.5	7.25
6 x 9	.66	.66	1	.66	4.66	7.33

Your settings can be changed if you don't like them. Once your book size and margin settings are in place, you can proceed with the writing or typing of the manuscript, making it camera-ready for your printer.

Photographs and Artwork

If the book will have illustrations, these, too, can be inserted from scanned images directly into the computer and onto the proper page of the manuscript.

To print photographs or artwork that is not solid black and white in your book, the printer needs "*halftones.* This is a process where the original photographs are "re-photographed" through a screen, resulting in a print made up of minute dots. The human eye then blends these dots together into a continuous tone.

Expect to pay $8 to $15 to have a halftone made of each of your photos, but the overall cost for an entire book is relatively inexpensive. Professionally scanned photos are generally far superior to those made by home scanners purchased at local computer supply stores, although home scanners too, are getting better and better in the quality they can produce.

Your book's printer can scan your photos and convert them into halftones at about the same price that graphics or copy shops will charge.

Use an organized method so the printer will know where each photo and caption will go in your book. One easy way is to number each photo with the page number, such as "p. 34", and number each caption with a corresponding number.

Quality of the printed photographs that appear in your book will depend upon the quality of the original. Printing plants can usually do some minor correction to make poor photos look better, but no one can make a really bad photo look good, let alone perfect.

Good quality color photos can also be reproduced as black and white halftones. The printing plant can reduce or enlarge photos to fit the space in which they are to be place.

Now that you have the mechanics in place, you can continue writing your book. Even before your manuscript is completed, there are a number of chores that need to be done. The first, and perhaps the main one, is to set up a company. Let's get to it!

Step 2

Setting Up Your Company

Naming Your Business

One of the first things you need to do is name your newly formed publishing company. It isn't necessary to wait until your book is finished to set up your company. In fact, the sooner you do it, the better, so you can get your stationery, bank accounts, and other necessities in order.

Naming your company can be the fun part of starting up a business. Believe me, you'll find enough other things involved in the process that aren't fun. As a self-publisher, you probably won't need the services of an attorney. However, if there are sticky issues involved, such as a complicated partnership, then you should consult one.

You have wide latitude in naming your enterprise as long as someone else doesn't already have the name.

Some authorities frown on the use of your own name as the business name. While perfectly legal, the use of your "family" name signifies to some that you are just a small operator. Also, if you ever sell the business, the name goes with it.

Don't choose a name that will limit your publishing potential. For instance, if you used "Children's Publishing Company" or "Just Animals Publishing", you might box yourself in to publishing only children's materials or books on animals.

When naming my own company, "Stagecoach Publishing", I mulled over a seemingly endless list of potential names. However, "Stagecoach" kept resounding in my head and even in my sleep. I finally said to myself, "If 'Stagecoach' just won't go away, I'll use it!"

Luckily for me, the name had not been usurped by anyone else, although there is a prominent bank that uses a stagecoach in its logo. I had, by this time, become so attached to the name I would have died if I couldn't have used it.

I've never been sorry for choosing the name. It seems to fit well with the type of books I write, which is primarily on California History. It is easy to remember, and carries a touch of class.

While there is that bank that uses a stagecoach in its logo, I feel their choice simply shows their good taste.

Once you've chosen your new publishing company's name, it is now time to make it official.

Making Your Company Legal

You've picked your company name, and need to register it. First, go to a public library and research the name you've chosen in *Books in Print and Literary Market Place.* Look also in your local telephone directory, to make sure no one else owns the name. If your choice is already taken, you'll simply have to choose another name.

If the name is not taken, your next move is to go to the county clerk's office and file a "DBA" ("doing business as") statement, letting the public know that you and your publishing company are one and the same.

The county clerk's office will advise you on any other steps to follow, which will include purchasing a legal ad in a local newspaper, which amounts to announcing that you're open for business. Any challengers to your new company are expected to come forward during the four-week period in which the ad runs.

You needn't choose an expensive daily newspaper in which to run your tiny legal ad. Any small weekly in your county will do the job just as well and for much less money.

Types of Business Structures

When forming a new publishing company, there are three types of business structures from which to choose: "sole proprietorship", "partnership", and "corporation".

Each type has its advantages, and if there is any doubt, you should certainly consult both a taxman and an attorney.

For the new self-publisher, a sole proprietorship is generally the best choice, as it simplifies bookkeeping and tax records.

A sole proprietorship means the business will be owned and operated by one person. In essence, when you become a sole proprietor you are simply becoming a self-employed individual. Some communities may require you to have a business license or permit.

The best place to find out exactly what you need to do to form a sole proprietorship is your county clerk's office. All the necessary paperwork will be there and you can fill out a DBA (*doing business as*) form on the spot.

The clerk's office will then advise you on the next steps to take to complete your business formation. As mentioned earlier, this will include taking out an advertisement in a local paper announcing your new business.

If you later want to upgrade from a sole proprietor to a C-Corporation or LLC (limited liability company) as your business grows and you wish to protect your assets, you can do so. This, too, would be accomplished through the county clerk's office.

The county clerk's office will notify you when your legal ad has run the proper four-week period if no objections have been voiced by readers of your legal ad or others who have now become aware of your intended enterprise. Once you get the County Clerk's approval, you are essentially in business and can claim the title of publisher.

Open A Business Bank Account

Now that you're in business, it is time to act like a businessman or businesswoman. You need a bank account under your business name and at least a simple accounting program. Accounting can actually be done on a simple check register, listing all your expenditures and detailing what was included in each purchase.

Stagecoach Publishing uses Quickbooks accounting software, published by Quicken. This allows the publisher to print invoices, statements, cash payments, and allows you to keep track of expenses. It also allows you to issue those dreaded return and credit memos for books that have been returned from bookstores. It provides invaluable records at tax time.

There is any number of expensive and inexpensive money managing software packages available that will do the same thing. A simple one will probably handle all that is needed for a first book publisher.

There are some who rely only on a checkbook register. This can certainly be adequate if proper notations are made for what the expenses were. Don't try to remember the transaction at the end of the year when you're filling out your tax return.

While an accounting software program isn't vital, it certainly lessens some of the headaches in bookkeeping.

Stationery and Business Cards

Letterhead stationery and business cards are something a new publisher will use a lot, especially in the first few months of starting the business.

If you own your own computer, or plan to, you can design your own letterhead with whatever word processing software you use. Copy shops and local printers can be of great help in designing and printing stationery and business cards.

Besides, many of them are in a similar position as the self-publisher. They will appreciate your business.

Stagecoach
   Publishing
Alton Pryor, Publisher
5360 Campcreek Loop
Roseville, CA. 95747
Phone: (916) 771-8166
stagecoachpublishing@surewest.net
www.stagecoachpublishing.com

The author designed the above letterhead for his publishing company on his computer, using Microsoft Word, the very same software he used to write his books. Not too bad for an amateur.

Getting All Your Numbers Together

ISBN or International Standard Book Number is one thing you want to get before you finish writing the manuscript. This is a ten-digit number that is printed on the copyright page (generally page four of your book) and on the bottom of the back cover, either above or below the bar code.

The easiest and quickest way to acquire an ISBN number is to go online: http://www.isbn.org, click on "U.S. Agency" and follow online instructions. There is a handling fee ($225 for regular processing) for a block of 10 ISBN numbers. It is also possible to get blocks of 100, 1000 and 10,000 numbers, but this probably will not apply to the reader of this book. For expedited handling, there will be an extra charge. All of the fees are spelled out in the "online" application form.

As a beginning publisher, a block of 10 numbers should serve you well. The first number is always used to designate the ISBN Logbook that is sent to you with your block of numbers. You have nine numbers left to begin your publishing enterprise.

You simply assign each book you publish a different number from your list. You don't have to select them in any order. Just don't use the same one on two different books. Record the number and the book title on the Logbook sent to you.

Stagecoach Publishing acquired its block of 10 ISBN numbers in 1997, and this current book is using the eighth number of the block. This means that my company can publish only one more book before having to reorder another block of ISBN numbers. (Remember one number was assigned to the ISBN logbook)

If you are curious as to what these numbers all mean, this information is available at the same web site from which you acquire the numbers. Suffice it to say, if you're going to be a book publisher, you absolutely must acquire an ISBN number.

Place your ISBN number on your title page (usually page 4 of your book) and on the back cover as part of the bar code. You can look on the title page and the back cover of this book and readily see how the ISBN number needs to be applied.

Online ordering at R.R. Bowker is safe, and applicants need not worry about their credit card numbers being misused.

To order your block of 10 ISBN numbers, go online to ISBN.org and follow the directions for applying. You will be asked to fill out a one-page form, submit a credit card number, and click a submit button. Within days, you should have your block of numbers with complete instructions on how to place them in your book.

Advance Book Information is another service provided by R.R. Bowker. By filling out their ABI form, your book will be listed in *Books in Print* and a number of other directories. The Books in Print directory is published in October of each year and is an important reference used by the book industry. One source says Advance Book Information is as important in generating book orders as the yellow pages are to local businessmen.

You should receive an Advance Book Information application with your block of ISBN numbers. Be sure to fill it out.

Library of Congress Control Number (LCCN)

This is a number that should also appear on the copyright page of your new book. This number is particularly important to libraries that might order your book.

The Library of Congress Control Number or LCCN is a number assigned by the Library of Congress. The Library of Congress control numbering system has had the same basic structure since its initial use in 1898. However, on January 1, 2001, the structure changed to accommodate a four-digit year. The new structure will apply to LCCNs assigned in 2001 forward.

To get your LCCN, log on to their web site:

www.loc.gov/marc/lccn.html

Simply follow the directions on the web site to acquire your number. I received the LCCN number for this book in about three days. It was sent to me by email by the Library of Congress.

Copyright

Your book is automatically Copyright protected under common law because you wrote and created it. However, it isn't copyright registered until you submit an application and fee.

Contact the Copyright Office, Library of Congress, 101 Independence Avenue, S.E., Washington, D.C. 20559-6000. You can also access information and fill out Form TX by going online at the Copyright Office's Web site: http://loc.gov/copyright.

Print a copyright notice on the title page even though it is not yet registered with the copyright office. You should register your book with the Copyright Office within three months of it coming off the press.

Check out any book to see how the copyright notice should read on your title page, which, by the way, is page four in most books. In this book, the copyright notice reads:

Copyright©2002 By Alton Pryor

The copyright is good for the life of the author plus 50 years. Your ownership of a copyright now makes your book a part of your estate.

Coping with Symbols in Your Manuscript

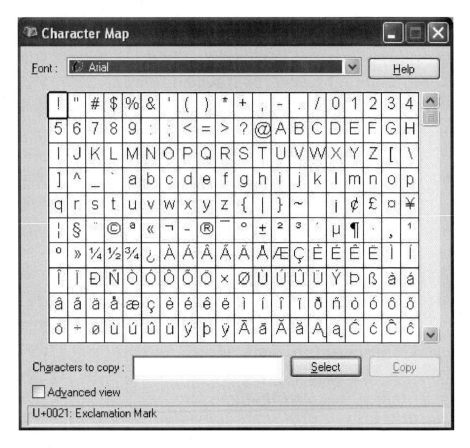

Word processors contain all those symbols that sometimes plague authors who want to insert them in their manuscripts but don't know how. On Microsoft Word, you can select a symbol from the Character Map.

There is another way, however.

Take the © or Copyright symbol for instance. You'll need it in every book you write. Just hold down the "Alt" key on your computer, type in the number of the symbol you want, and when you release the "Alt" key, the desired symbol will appear where your cursor is located. A list of Symbol Access Numbers is listed on the next page.

È	0200	Ê	0202	Ï	0207
‰	0137	Ë	0203	Ò	0210
™	0153	Î	0206	Õ	0213
©	0169	Ñ	0209	Ù	0217
®	0174	Ô	0212	Ü	0220
±	0177	Ø	0216	ß	0223
½	0189	Û	0219	â	0226
À	0192	Þ	0222	å	0229
Æ	0198	á	0225	è	0232
É	0201	ä	0228	ë	0235
~	0126	ç	0231	î	0238
œ	0156	ê	0234	ñ	0241
§	0167	í	0237	ó	0244
µ	0181	ð	0240	÷	0247
°	0176	ó	0243	ú	0250
¾	0190	ö	0246	ý	0253
Á	0193	ù	0249	Í	0205
Ä	0196	ü	0252	Ð	0208
Ç	0199	Ì	0204	Ó	0211
µ	0181	Ö	0214	Ú	0218
Ý	0221	à	0224	ã	0227
æ	0230	é	0233	ì	0236
ï	0239	ò	0242	õ	0245
ø	0248	û	0251	þ	0254

Don't Forget the Bar code

The Bookland EAN bar code is another item that is absolutely necessary to enable you to sell your book efficiently. A bar code allows a scanning device to identify the title, ISBN number, and the price of the book. A bar code is relatively easy to get.

On mass-market paperback books, such as sold in supermarkets as well as bookstores, an additional bar code, called the Universal Product Code or (UPC) is needed. To obtain a UPC bar code, contact the Uniform Code Council at its web site: www.uccouncil.org.

Their web site fully explains the procedure for obtaining the Price Point UPC with ISBN add-on Code.

Sometimes, the book's printer can apply the code (usually at a small charge). Stagecoach Publishing purchased its own bar code software program off the Internet and it has proven to be both satisfactory and convenient. It cost a mere $35 for the software and the time saved in getting a new bar code is well worth the price.

Owning your own software program is especially helpful if it is ever necessary to raise the price of a book because of increased printing costs. A new bar code can easily be printed on adhesive labels and applied over the old bar code on the back cover of books already in your inventory.

Page and Cover Design

Remember, your cover is your "Billboard". It is the cover that most likely carries the greatest influence on getting a customer to pick up your book in the first place. Good covers probably sell more books than good content, but it's certainly best to have both.

You can't spend too much time in composing a good book title. Keep in mind that the title must grab the buyers' attention but it also should address the potential market of the book.

"How to Make One Million in A Year," is infinitely better than a title stating, "Get Rich Quick."

While it may sound crass, the simple truth is that a book's title has one purpose, and that is: "To sell your book." To do so, the title still must convey some sense of what the book is about.

The title of my first book, "Little Known Tales in California History," has been responsible for the bulk of its sales. In a bookstore, the title is almost an "impulse" buy. Thankfully, my readers have felt that the contents lived up to the title.

The Back Cover

Almost as important as the cover is the "back cover". In a bookstore, books are frequently displayed with only their spines in a readable position. Once the reader decides to pick up the book, the first few seconds will be devoted to the cover.

Then, most readers will flip it over and read the back cover. Make sure that the copy on your back cover sizzles and grabs the reader's attention. If the back cover content sparks his interest, he or she will very likely buy the book. If the book's title and the copy on the back cover are dull and unconvincing, you very likely will not make the sale.

Before writing your back cover copy, go to a bookstore and look over books in the same category as yours. See what the writer has to say on the back cover. As you read the back cover material, ask yourself if it makes you want to purchase the book.

It is important to let your potential buyer know what he will gain by purchasing your book. Too many authors are weak and uninspiring in their back cover sales copy. You can't spend too much time writing the copy for your back cover. It will be the best, or worst, salesman for your book, depending on what you've written.

At the very top, left corner, of your back cover, you must have a subject code. The Book Industry Systems Advisory Committee has developed a list of 2,000 subjects and subject codes to be used to describe the contents of a specific title.

You will find a list of the General Headings for each of the 46 major categories located on the back of the Advanced Book Information Form that you need to fill out.

These categories help booksellers when they are deciding where to stock your book. See next page for the list.

Here are the 46 most popular subject headings:

Antiques/Collectibles
Architecture
Biography/Autobiography/Letters
Business/Economics/Finance
Computer Technology & Software
Cookbooks & Cookery
Crafts & Hobbies
Current Affairs
Drama
Education & Teaching
Family/Child Care/Relationships
Fiction/Literature
Foreign Language Instruction & Reference
Games
Gardening & Horticulture
Health & Fitness
History
Home Improvement & Construction
Humor
Language Arts
Law
Literary Criticism & Essays

Mathematics
Medical/Nursing/Home Care
Music
Nature & Natural History
Occultism/Parapsychology
Performing Arts
Pets & Pet Care
Philosophy
Photography
Poetry
Political Science & Government
Psychology/Psychiatry
Reference
Religion/Bibles
Science
Self-Actualizatlon/Self-Help
Social Sciences
Sports & Recreation
Study Aids
Technology & Industrial Arts
Transportation
Travel & Travel Guides
True Crime

If your title doesn't fit into any of these categories, contact:

R.R. Bowker Data Collection Center
P.O. Box 6000-0103
Oldsmar, FL 34677-0103
(800) 521-8100 (Reed Reference)
email: info@reedref.com

The Spine

On the spine of the book, place the title and the name of the author (that is, your name). Some bookstores and book distributors almost demand that your book contain a spine if they are going to carry it. DO NOT PUBLISH WITHOUT ONE.

Since book buyers purchase books based on content or by author, it isn't necessary to put the name of your self-publishing company on the spine. Since your company is new, it's unlikely anyone outside your closest friends and family would recognize it anyway.

Calculate the Spine Width

If you're using a cover designer, you will have to provide he or she with information on how wide the spine should be. There is a method that easily determines the width of the spine.

Here's How:

1. Count the number of pages in your book. Include the front and back cover as well as any blank pages. When you agree the printer on the weight of the paper you will use in your book, make note of the PPI (Pages Per Inch).

2. Divide the number of pages by the PPI. For instance, 200 pages divided by 500 ppi stock would give you .40.

3. This means the type on your spine must fit onto a spine that is slightly under one-half inch thick.

Paper weights are not always the same. You can't depend upon a 50-pound paper being 500 DPI.

Step 3

Printing Your Book

Getting Estimates

Printing costs are one of the most important aspects of getting your book published. Printing costs make up by far the highest cost of publishing a book, unless you splurge on a big marketing campaign, and consequently play a big role in setting the retail price at which the book will be sold.

Get several estimates to get your book printed. I seldom seek less than six printing bids on a new book. In getting the estimates, make sure you give the various printers being solicited the exact same information. It is not fair to a printer to be bidding on different specifications than his competitors are estimating.

One self-publishing source suggests getting bids from three companies for 1,000 copies. This might work, but I personally like to know what the unit price is on 1,000 copies, 2,000 and 3,000 books. The difference can sometimes be staggering.

It is possible to submit RQFs (request for quotation) on the web site of most printers, and even fill out the request right online. You will be asked to submit your specifications for the number of pages in your book, the paper stock, ink (grayscale or color) and cover information. The form usually lists any extra charges, such as setup and shipping.

Keep in mind that shipping from a printing plant close to your place of business can be considerably less expensive than from a printing plant located across the country. The difference in shipping costs could be the item that might sway your decision in choosing a printer.

Information Needed for Printer Estimate

Trim Size:
- ☐ 5-1/2 x 8-1/2
- ☐ 6x9
- ☐ 7x10
- ☐ 8-1/2 x 11
- ☐ Other [_____]

Quantity:
- ☐ 500
- ☐ 1000
- ☐ 3000
- ☐ 5000
- ☐ 10000
- ☐ Other:

Page Count:
(page count must be divisible by 4)

[_____]

Text art supplied as:
- ○ Camera ready
- ○ Disk To Film
- ○ Full typesetting
- ○ Typesetting from disk

- ○ Negatives provided
- ○ Internet submission

Inside text prints:

- ○ Black ink throughout (1/1)
- ○ Black + 1 PMS / 2 sides
- ○ Black + 2 PMS / 2 sides

Does the inside text bleed?:
[No ▼]

Text stock:

- ○ 50# offset
- ○ 55# book, cream
- ○ 60# offset
- ○ 70# offset

Number of halftones: *If your book requires duotones or color separations please contact us.*

[_____]

Cover art provided as:

- ○ Camera ready
- ○ Disk to film
- ○ Composite film with matchprint
- ○ Composite film without matchprint
- ○ CPBM to typeset

Outside cover prints:

- ○ 4 color process
- ○ Black + 3 PMS
- ○ Black + 2 PMS
- ○ Black + 1 PMS
- ○ Black ink only
- ○ 4 PMS colors
- ○ 3 PMS colors
- ○ 2 PMS colors
- ○ 1 PMS color

Cover finish:

- ○ Gloss lamination
- ○ Matte lamination

- ○ Varnish
- ○ UV coating

Cover stock:

- ○ 10 pt C1S
- ○ 12 pt C1S

- ○ Perfect-bound
- ○ Saddlestitch (100 pgs or less)
- ○ GBC binding
- ○ Plasticoil binding
- ○ Wire-o binding

Would you like your books shrinkwrapped?:

- ○ Yes
- ⦿ No

If so, how many per package?

[   ]

Let's saunter through the printing estimate request form. As mentioned earlier, there are four basic trim sizes: 4 1/4 x 7 inches; 5 1/2 x 8 1/2 inches; 6 x 9, inches; and 8 1/2 x 11 inches.

The quantity you order depends on the printing estimate you get. Get estimates for one, two, and three thousand copies and see the difference. If you think you can sell three thousand, go for it.

If you want to test market, use a "Print on Demand" printer and order fewer books, anywhere from 25 to 100 should get the information you need. Expect to pay a lot more per book for Print on Demand versions, but it may be worth it for the marketing information you get back.

For page count, do no include the front and back cover or the cover insides. The page count is simply the total number of pages in your book. If you set up your book as suggested, your word processor will tell you immediately the number of pages of your finished product.

If you are following this manual, your answer to Text Art Supplied will probably be "Camera Ready". Otherwise, simply select another choice.

Inside text prints: Generally this will be black ink throughout.

The question about inside text prints will normally be "Black Ink Throughout" (1/1)

For "Does Inside Text Bleed?" simply answer yes or no. If photos do bleed, you'll pay more.

Under proofs, "Blueline" will serve your purpose.

Text stock: check 50-pound offset for most estimates. The paper stock is an issue that should be discussed with your printer. He can explain to you the differences.

Under the number of halftones, simply list the number of photographs being included.

For the question on cover prints, if you are using four colors on your cover, check that box. If you have only black and one color, insert 2.

Inside cover prints are probably not a part of your book. The inside cover will normally be blank (or white).

Cover finish: discuss this with your printer. At a minimum you will want UV coating to protect your book. Gloss and matte laminations will give added protection to the cover.

Most cover stock answers will be 10 pt. C1S (coated one side).

Under binding, unless you are publishing a cookbook, which you would want to lie flat when opened, check the "perfect binding" box. If you think you would want another type of binding, discuss it with the printer.

Packaging: If your books are individually wrapped, they will cost you more. The number of books per carton is usually based on the size of your book. Most cartons should end up weighing about 30 pounds. Ask your printer for his suggestions.

Print On Demand

Print on demand (POD) is a relatively new technology that allows a complete book to be printed and bound in a matter of minutes. Books can therefore be produced as ordered or in small lots (rather than in runs of several thousand, as in traditional printing).

POD books cost more per unit to produce than books produced by means of a traditional print run on a web press. For this reason, you'll never see a POD book that's mass-market paperback-size (it couldn't be priced at a level competitive with commercially-produced mass markets and allow the publisher to make a profit). You will seldom see a hardback POD book for the same reason, cost. The vast majority of POD books are trade paperback-size.

As a first-time self-publisher, you might want to consider using POD printing technology to "test market" your new book. The books will cost you more per unit, but if you only have to order 25 to 100 copies to see how it's going to fly, it might be worth the extra cost.

I personally have used POD printing on three of my books when I didn't feel I wanted two or three thousand books stacked up in my garage.

POD technology has a number of applications. Commercial publishers use it when they can't justify the expense of producing and warehousing a traditional print run. For instance, POD allows a publisher to keep lower-selling books and/or their backlists available, without warehousing them.

Some independent publishers use POD as a more economical publishing model, trading higher up-front costs and smaller profits for convenience and less initial investment. Last but not least, there's the growing number of fee-based POD publishing services that provide a service that's similar--but not identical--to self-publishing.

It's important to remember that in and of itself, POD is not a publishing paradigm. It's merely a technology, used in different ways by different publishers to accomplish a variety of goals.

It's important to find a printer with whom you feel comfortable, whether it is a convention printer with huge web presses, or a small POD firm. Sometimes you may want to use a printer you like even if he might not be the absolute lowest bidder. There are too many problem areas that can pop up during the production process, and you want someone that will help smooth out these wrinkles.

Printers, too, are looking for your repeat business. This compels them to do the best job of producing your book that they can so as to keep you in their fold.

How Many Should You Print?

Predicting how a book is going to fly in the market place has perplexed both self-publishers as well as the giant publishing houses. It would be nice to have 20/20 hindsight, but after publishing my first seven books, I've given up guessing just what will catch on.

I do know that compelling and interesting covers sell books. Also, the material on the back cover will help sell books. You need a good table of contents and if the book warrants it, an index.

Printing 1,000 books is a lot more expensive per book than printing 10,000. This translates into less profit per book. But if you have 9000 of the books left over after your big book run, you've taken a gamble that didn't pay off.

Remember, too, that if you need a second printing, the price will be less (if you use the same printer) because most of the setup costs were paid for in the first print run.

Pricing Your Book

There may be only one thing worse for a publisher than to "over-price" his book. That is to "under-price" it.

To arrive at a price necessary to make a profit, the publisher must take into account the various discounts he must offer to book wholesalers, distributors, independent bookstores, gift shops and other customers.

It is necessary also, to keep the price low enough that you don't encounter customer price resistance. Finding the proper formula is not always easy.

A book distributor will demand a 55 percent or higher discount off the retail price for the "privilege" of carrying your book. Bookstores will generally settle for a 40 percent discount, and gift shops might agree to carry the book at a 50 percent discount. Gift shop sales, as well as many bookstore sales will be in very small volumes.

Consignments

As a newcomer to the scene when my first book, "Little Known Tales in California History", hit the market, I felt allowing bookstores to carry the book on consignment was necessary.

I've since discontinued all consignment accounts. Why should you bankroll the bookstore? From a business point of view, what incentive does the bookstore have to feature your book when he can carry it for nothing? The store is going to feature the book for which it had to pay hard cash.

Most important in my decision to stop consigning books, however, was the fact that no bookstore carrying my book on consignment ever voluntarily paid for the books it sold. It required sending and resending statements and urgent requests for payment. Failing to be paid for six months or more became a common and frustrating headache. There are some consignment accounts I've never been able to collect.

Worse, consignment accounts are bookkeeping nightmares. You may lose some sales by not placing your books on consignment; the loss is compensated by the elimination of the problems associated with consignments.

Shipping Costs

It's important to factor in shipping costs, both from the printer for your new books, as well as the shipping cost for those going to your book wholesalers and distributors. Both distributors and wholesalers expect the publisher to pick up the shipping costs on their orders.

The retail price, which is going to be printed on the bar code, is generally set at five to eight times production costs, which mainly includes printing and shipping from the printer to your place of business. If you have other costs, such as typesetting, these should be factored in as well.

It is virtually impossible to put a proper price on your new book until you know the costs involved. These costs include printing, office supplies, and any other costs involved. If you intend to launch an advertising campaign for your book, these costs, too, should be included.

Be aware that you don't want to price yourself out of business. First time self-publishers are more likely to price their first book too low rather than too high. It seems, at first, important to get the book out there at any cost.

The general formula for self-publishers of from five to eight times the first-run production costs seems to work pretty well. Stagecoach Publishing typically prices its books at the lower end of this formula. I like to adhere to the advice of a good friend: "You'll never go broke making a profit." He neglected to tell me that sometimes you'd get close.

I will inform you that I have had to bite the bullet and raise the price on some of my books after the first, second or third printings. Luckily, this can be done quite easily as I purchased a bar code program that will quickly print new prices and a correct bar code onto labels that can cover the old bar code labels.

Mass marketing experts have proven that a $9.95 price is somehow much more attractive than an even $10 price; a

$14.95 price is more attractive than a $15 price, and $19.95 items sell better than $20 items.

List Your Mistakes

If the first printing of your book doesn't contain any errors, you are indeed one good editor. I have failed to see any book that didn't have a few errors even in some of its reprints.

You naturally will want to correct any errors that you see, and make a list of those that readers call to your attention. When it comes time to reprint, you can make a simple correction on your computer and have your printer insert the corrected page in its proper place. (He may charge a small fee for this)

Encourage readers to write or email you with any typographical errors or other mistakes they uncover in your book. Most will welcome the chance to be helpful.

Step 4

Marketing your book

The Job Most Publishers and Authors Hate

Even though the publisher is paying whopping discounts to book wholesalers and distributors, most, if not all the work of marketing a book will fall on the self-publisher's shoulders.

It is up to the self-publisher to send out news releases, call on newspapers, radio and television stations and, yes, even bookstores, which your distributors might overlook. If you are like most self-publishers, your duties will also include bookkeeping, addressing shipping labels, and packaging whatever orders you might receive. You may also find that you are the sweeper, the cleaner, and the window-washer for your little publishing domain.

Contact your local newspapers, including the weeklies and free handout newspapers to see if they might do an interview a book review, and perhaps use a photo.

Send copies of your book to appropriate publications for their book review sections.

Book Distributors and Wholesalers

One would at first assume a distributor that demands a 55 percent discount off the retail price of a book he wants to handle would be more involved in the book's marketing. It hardly ever happens. All too frequently, a book distributor or wholesaler is simply an order taker, but you'll find it's necessary to use them if you're going to sell to bookstores.

While there is a difference in book distributors and book wholesalers, for our discussion here, we will refer to both as distributors. Let me emphasize, there are good book distributors as well as bad book distributors, but it seems to be a trial and error process to determine which is which.

My biggest orders have come from Costco Stores. Getting into Costco Stores wasn't just a happenstance affair, however. When my first book, "Little Known Tales in California History" came out in 1997, I personally went to my local Costco and asked the manager for the name and address of the book buyer. (The main Costco office is located in Issaquah, WA.)

I immediately wrote a cover letter, including the names of a couple of my book distributors. Along with a cover letter, I included a review copy of the book.

It was several months before I heard anything, but one day I received a phone call from Sun Belt Publications, 1250 Fayette St., El Cajon, California. The buyer said he needed 4,704 books, the largest single order I had ever received.

I was a little stunned, and even considered that it might be a "crank call". The buyer laughed and said, "I'm prepared to fax you a purchase order."

My immediate reply was, "Please do!"

The angel for publishers must have been really shining that week. In a couple of days, I again received a call from Sunbelt Publications, saying that an additional 1,680 books was needed. The thing that prompted the additional order was that Costco had decided to place one carton of books in each of its California stores.

You can imagine how I scurried to get the order filled. As luck would have it, I was in the process of getting my first reprint of "Little Known Tales in California History". I was able to call the printer and tack on another 7,000 books to the order to fulfill Costco's order.

The books sold well. During that first Costco sale, I received fewer than 35 copies back, and these were copies that had been damaged in shipment.

Stagecoach Publishing uses about eight different book distributors in an attempt to cover all bases. Luckily, one of my distributors, American Books West, at 1831 Industrial Way, Sanger, California, 93657, has done a lot of legwork in getting three of my books placed again in Costco Stores. (My first sale to Costco occurred before I became connected with American West Books.)

One of the things I learned through a little research is that Costco will generally not buy from a publisher with only a few titles. They insist on going through a book distributor or wholesaler.

Their reasoning is economics. They would rather write a single check for a large number of titles, than several checks to a number of publishers from whom they might only purchase a book or two.

Some bookstores, too, will not purchase books directly from a self-publisher. They generally want to buy from one of the major distributors or wholesalers, such as Ingram Book Company or Baker & Taylor.

If you are new to self-publishing, and you probably are if you're reading this book, don't faint when you are informed of the distributors' take. Their demand for a 55 percent discount off your book's retail price is pretty much standard. (There are some distributors who might want more and may even demand exclusivity with your book.)

While I personally don't care to give a distributor exclusive rights to distribute my books, there can be advantages to doing so. Giving a distributor exclusive rights to handle book trade sales will free you up to spend your time marketing to the gift trade, catalog sales, and other potential outlets for your books.

Steal a Page from the Giants

Large publishing houses often schedule appearances by authors to do bookstore signings. You, as a self-publisher, especially if you are a publisher/author, can make use of this tool to move books.

This is a good chance to meet your readers. Try to have a speech dealing with your book and its subject matter. This will help to attract an audience. Most bookstore personnel will welcome chances to present local authors in their stores, and such appearances nearly always result in the store ordering extra books.

Reaching the Library and School Market

Getting into the library and public school market has been one of the toughest sells for Stagecoach Publishing. Even though two of my books received approval for use in grades four through eight by the California Department of Education, and were added to the department's web site, few sales resulted.

To be completely honest, I feel that my failure to penetrate these markets were probably my own fault, due to not knowing how to get the ear of the proper persons. I haven't given up on these markets, but it is a hard sell.

The American Library Association estimates there are more than 120,000 libraries in the U.S. Wouldn't it be nice just to sell a single book to each one? Libraries account for more than ten percent of all book sales in the country.

In his book, "The Complete Guide to Book Marketing," author David Cole says libraries spend some $1.6 billion annually on books alone. They spend another $3.4 billion on new materials, including books, subscriptions, and various formats for audio and video products.

"This is clearly a market worth attending to," said Cole. Cole suggests author-publishers can do some things to make their books more attractive to libraries.

Libraries focus on books in their collections as tools to give its clientele information on a myriad of topics. Cole said libraries like to see a clear title and subtitle, a well-organized table of contents, and an index. Including these features in your book will help get librarians attention.

Librarians are aware of the cost of processing books. An author-publisher can make their job easier by securing a Library of Congress catalog card number known as a PCN, or preassigned card number.

Fill out the Advance Book Information and Books in Print forms you receive from R.R. Bowker when you get your ISBN numbers. These help keep libraries informed of your book or books.

Develop a Mailing List

Don't make the mistake that I did with my first book. While I had the names of the people that had purchased my book on my computer, I failed to develop a list in a methodical manner. A computer crash sent my fledgling sales information down to whatever cemetery computer documents go after death.

If you use good bookkeeping software, your mailing list is pretty much automatically kept intact. Make sure you back up this information frequently. Quickbooks, which I use for my accounting, does a great job, even to the point of reminding you about frequent backups.

You may say to yourself that you won't need the names of these people again. Believe me, you'll be kicking yourself later if you don't keep a buyer's list. Your previous book's buyer list will be like money in the bank when you write a second book. If your first book is a success, you are virtually certain to want to do another.

Working Arts and Craft Shows

One of my best sales outlets has been Art and Craft fairs that are seemingly held someplace every weekend of the year. You will find at first that a lot of these events will not be worth returning to the next year. But you won't know until you give them a try.

If you plan on selling at craft fairs, one piece of equipment is almost vital, and that is an easy to erect canopy from which to work, such as an "EZ-UP" or a "Caravan" awning. Many events demand that awnings be white canvas, rather than multi-colored, so you might want to keep this in mind if you buy one.

You'll quickly learn which events are your most lucrative for sales. There are craft fair guides that will list the dates, locations and costs of the various craft fairs. A lot of craft fair and other event information can be found on the Internet.

Many will have their own web sites and will even allow you to fill out an application right online, paying for the space fee by a secure credit card.

My First Craft Fair

I'll never forget my first craft fair. It occurred only two months after my first book was published. I was late getting my application in for the craft show (I hardly knew there were such affairs), and consequently didn't get to pick a preferred booth site.

My space was located at the very end of the street on which the craft show was held. Vendors lined Sutter Street for about five blocks down "Old Town" in Folsom, California. There were literally hundreds of vendors there, and my booth was located not only at the end of the street, but next to a fireplug. I just knew the day would be a lost cause.

As luck would have it, craft show customers had to park just around the corner from my booth. They passed me walking into the craft show, and they passed me again walking out. On top of that, they were shopping for Christmas gifts and my book apparently "filled the Christmas stocking" for many of them.

Two hours into the show, I had to call my wife to bring more books. It turned into one of the better shows I've ever done, and I still go there each December.

The types of marketing you do will naturally depend on the nature of your book. If your book is a fiction novel, it probably won't find a good buying market in a craft show.

That doesn't mean that you can't set up book signing events on your own that might attract buyers. Bookstores will generally go overboard to set up such a signing for a local author.

Don't overlook gift shops and other retail outlets to do the same thing. They naturally welcome any added publicity you generate. You will probably be expected to send newspaper, television and radio media a news release announcing such book signing events, and hope they will use it.

Draft A Good Speech

If you can become something of an expert on a topic, you will be desired as a speaker. If your book is a self-help type book, you're in luck. This may be the hottest area in the book market.

Online Bookstores

You will want to contact online booksellers and get your book listed. It's easier than you might think. Send each of them copies of your cover and back cover material, a table of contents, and a news release.

You can get addresses and other pertinent information by logging on, and clicking the "Information for Publishers" box that is supplied. Here is a listing of online booksellers:

www.amazon.com
www.bn.com
www.borders.com
www.booksamillion.com

If you don't toot your horn, you can bet there are few others who will. Publicity can be a great equalizer for the self-publisher and little known or unknown-writer.

Book buyers are avid readers of book review pages. Book reviewers actually carry a lot of clout when you realize it is the reviewers who decide which of the 135 titles published each day will get reviewed.

You may feel that providing too many review copies is too costly. Don't! Provide the copies and write them off as the cost of doing business. You never know when that one choice review will result is a spate of sales.

Librarians especially depend upon book reviews to make their buying decisions. Acquisition librarians don't have the time to read and evaluate all the new books.

And don't overlook your friendly hometown newspaper. As a local author, you will be something of a celebrity in the eyes of the newspaper staff and its readers. Make a trip to the desk of the managing editor and present him a copy. He'll likely assign a photographer to shoot your picture.

Step 5

Your Publishing Calendar

(Author's Note: I suggest you place a check mark in front of each of the following items as they are completed.

1. Name Your Company: Decide what you want to name your company. One of your first orders of business is to go to your County Clerk's office and file a fictitious name statement.

2. Place Legal Ad in Local Paper: Take out a legal ad in a local newspaper, announcing that you are operating under the name you've chosen. The newspaper will have the necessary forms and information. It isn't necessary to use the most widely circulated or expensive newspaper for this ad. It does have to be a newspaper in your county, but a weekly will do just as well as a daily.

3. Order Office Supplies: Since you're in business, you're going to need some requisite office supplies. These include business cards, letterheads, and envelopes. Don't forget the stamps.

4. Order Copyright Forms: Go online to the Library of Congress at www.loc.gov/copyright/ and download the applicable copyright forms. You will mail these with a copy of your finished book. You especially want form TX with the appropriate instructions. If you aren't

able to go online, you can contact the Copyright office by phone between 8:30 a.m. and 5 p.m. eastern time: (202) 707-3000.

5. Go Online to R.R. Bowker: This is a company you're going to deal with a lot. You will get a number of forms from Bowker, including one for a Cataloging in Publication (CIP) number; and Books in Print form. The most important of all is to get your block of ISBN numbers. As soon as your block of numbers come in the mail, choose one of them (you can pick any of the numbers, not necessarily in numerical order). You can apply and pay for the ISBN number online. Most of the forms can be downloaded from: www.bowker.com.

6. Your Book's Cover: If you haven't already completed a cover design, don't wait until your book is finished to do so. If you're using a graphic designer or other artist, they will need some leeway to design your cover.

7. Get Printer Bids: As soon as you have an inkling as to how many pages you will have in your book, start soliciting printer bids. You'll find a long list of book manufacturers in the resource section in the back of this book.

8. Get LCCN from Library of Congress: To get your LCCN, log on to their web site: www.loc.gov/marc/lccn.html
Simply follow the directions on the web site to acquire your number. I received the LCCN number for this book in about three days. It was sent to me by email by the Library of Congress.

9. Write A News Release: As your book is nearing completion, it is not too early to let the public know it has arrived. You want to spend some time on your release. Try to grab the readers' attention with your first sentence, and keep them hanging on as long as you can. Keep the news release to one double-spaced typewritten page.

10. Get Shipping Supplies: When your book finally arrives from the printer you will need padded shipping envelopes and shipping boxes. Don't be careless in packaging your books. Poorly packaged books will not only make you look cheap, but will likely result in the return of damaged books as well.

Hopefully, everything is ready for the arrival of your book. You've made room in your garage to store those that haven't already been sold; if not, you should have. If your book has been well prepared, you may be amazed at the pace they will disappear from your garage and you have to order a reprint.

Self-Publishing Resources

Books on Self-Publishing

The Self-Publishing Manual: How to Write, Print and Sell Your Own Book, Dan Poynter, Para Publishing.

The Complete guide to Self-Publishing: Everything You Need to Know to Write, Publish, Promote and Sell Your Own Book, Tom and Marilyn Ross, Writer's Digest Books.

How to Publish a Book and Sell a Million copies, Ted Nicholas, Dearborn Financial Publishing.

The Prepublishing Handbook: What You Should Know Before You Publish Your First Book, Patricia J. Bell, Cat's-Paw Press.

A Simple Guide to Self-Publishing: A Time and Money-Saving Handbook to Printing, Distributing and Promoting Your Own Book, Mark Ortman, Wise Owl Books.

Publishing Basics: A Guide for the Small Press and Independent Publisher, Robert Bowie Johnson, Jr., RJ Communications, LLC.

Smart Self-Publishing: An Author's Guide to Producing a Marketable Book, Linda and Jim Salisbury, Tabby House.

The Complete Guide to Book Marketing, David Cole, Allworth Press.

Business and Legal Forms for Authors & Self-Publishers, Tad Crawford, Allworth Press.

Book Printers

(This list is adapted from John Kremer's Book Marketing Website: www.bookmarket.com.)

You can find many others on the Internet and in Literary Market Place, available at your local library. Literary Market Place is a book that is well worth a look for a variety of resources.

Amica International, 844 Industry Drive, Seattle WA 98188; 206-575-2740; Fax: 206-575-2832. Email: amica@ix.netcom.com. They offer high-end, sheet fed printing of full-color art books, coffee-table books, 500+ page academic textbooks as well as catalogs, calendars, greeting cards, posters, and magazines.

The Argus Press, 7440 Natchez Avenue, Niles IL 60714-3869; 847-647-7800; 800-445-6528; Fax: 847-647-1709. A division of Master Graphics, they print books (5%) and directories (4%) in quantities up to 200,000.

Armstrong Industries Corporation, 065-665-8527; Fax: 065-665-8665. Email: savictor@armstrong.com.sg. Singapore book printers with a printing plant in China. "We believe we can offer our printing services with top quality and at very competitive prices. We accept both short and long run publications for newsletters, books, journals as well as magazines."

The Art Litho Co., 3500 Marmenco Court, Baltimore MD 21230; 410-789-5300; Fax: 410-789-7550. 10% of their business is printing books, especially in color. They outsource binding.

Artech Printing, 10100 Science Drive, Sturtevant WI 53177; 262-619-8900; 877-317-3400; Fax: 262-635-3450. Full service printing and binding, plus shipping, distribution, warehousing, etc. Specializes in full-color board books.

Asia Pacific Offset, 255 Lafayette Street #703, New York NY 10012; 212-941-8300; 800-756-6857; Fax: 212-941-9810. 21 Columbus Avenue #231, San Francisco CA 94111; 415-433-3488; 800-756-2309; Fax: 415-433-3489. Print brokers for 20 of the best color separators and printers in Hong Kong and China. Specializes in full-color printing. .

Aware Book Group, Two Worth Circle #2, Johnson City TN 37601; 800-994-0409; Fax: 800-979-0701. Email: abg@awareltd.com. From 250 to 30,000 copies. Specializes in short-run color books, including juvenile books.

Automated Graphic Systems, 4590 Graphics Drive, White Plains MD 20695; 301-843-6339; 800-678-8760; Fax: 301-843-6339. Email: info@ags.com. Ohio Office: 8107 Bavaria Road, Macedonia OH 44056; 330-963-7770; 800-362-6134; Fax: 330-963-7771. Owned by Consolidated Graphics.

Bang Printing, 1473 Highway 18 E, P O Box 587, Brainerd MN 56401; 218-829-2877; 800-328-0450; Fax: 218-829-7145. Email: chrisk@twwn.com.

Banta Book Group, Curtis Reed Plaza, 225 Main Street, P O Box 8003, Menasha WI 54952-8003; 920-751-7771; 800-291-1171; Fax: 920-751-7362. They print books and software manuals. They now also provide on-demand printing as well as regular printing. Call their 800 number to get a free subscription to their *News Brief* newsletter as well as a copy of their *Technovation Handbook*.

Batson Printing, 195 Michigan Street, Benton Harbor MI 49022; 616-926-6011; 800-926-3418; Fax: 616-926-6238.

Bay Port Press, 645-D Marsat Court, Chula Vista CA 91911-4649; 619-429-0100; 800-994-7737; Fax: 619-429-0199. Since 1978, they've been printing books, catalogs, directories, and manuals.

Bertelsmann Industry Services, Western Sales Office, 28210 North Avenue Stanford, Valencia CA 91355-1111; 800-223-1478; 888-564-0001; Fax: 661-775-4745. Email: bsimarketing@bisus.com. Bertelsmann Services, C Penny Callmeyer, Director, Business Development, 7485 Rush River Drive #710 PMB #301, Sacramento CA 95831; 888-564-0001; Fax: 916-924-3766. Email: penny.callmeyer@bisus.com. Main plant: Brentwood TN; 615-661-6367. Produces books, manuals, catalogs, and directories. Otabind lay-flat binding.

Berryville Graphics, 25 Jack Enders Boulevard, Berryville VA 22611; 540-955-9251; 800-382-7249; Fax: 540-955-2633. A division of Bertelsmann. 95% of their business is printing books.

Bethany Press, Marketing Director, 6820 West 115th Street, Bloomington MN 55438; 612-914-7417; 888-717-7400; Fax: 612-914-7410. Email: info@bethanypress.com. A division of a religious publisher, this printer has been in business for more than 50 years. Bethany Press International is a full-service perfect-bound book manufacturer for the Christian marketplace.

Bindagraphics, 2701 Wilmarco Avenue, Baltimore MD 21223; 410-362-7200; 800-326-0300; Fax: 410-362-7233. 27% of their business is in printing books.

Donald Blyler Offset, 1621 Willow Street, Lebanon PA 17042; 717-272-5656; Fax: 717-272-6263. Email: dbo@nbn.net. 10% of their business is in printing books and directories.

Book-Mart Press, 2001 42nd Street, North Bergen NJ 07047; 201-864-1887; 212-594-3344; Fax: 201-864-7559. A subsidiary of Courier Corporation. Prints paperback and hardcover.

BookMasters, 2541 Ashland Road, P O Box 2139, Mansfield OH 44905; 419-589-5100; 800-537-6727; Fax: 419-589-4040. Email: info@bookmaster.com. Offers prepress, printing, storage, fulfillment, and Internet sales.

Books Just Books, 51 East 42nd Street, New York City NY 10017; 800-621-2556. Email: Ron@rjc-lcc.com. Allows you to get book quotes online.

Books on Demand, CSS Publishing Company, 517 S Main Street, Lima OH 45804; 419-227-1818; 800-241-4056; Fax: 419-228-9184. Email: bod@csspub.com. They do both offset and on-demand printing of books, with hardcover, perfect-bound, saddlestiched, and comb bindings.

Boyd Printing, 49 Sheridan Avenue, Albany NY 12210; 518-436-9686; 800-877-2693; Fax: 518-436-7433. 10% of their business is in printing books in 10,000 plus quantities.

Brenneman Printing, 1909 Olde Homestead Lane, P O Box 11147, Lancaster PA 17605-1147; 717-299-2847; Fax: 717-299-4965. 20% of their business is in printing books and directories.

C&M Press, 4825 Nome Street, Denver CO 80239; 303-375-9922; Fax: 303-375-8699. Email: beth@cmpress.com. 90% of their business is in printing books and directories in runs under 10,000.

Carvajal International, 901 Ponce De Leon Boulevard #901, Coral Gables FL 33134; 305-448-6875; 800-622-6657; Fax: 305-448-9942. The U.S. office for a Columbian book printer, specialists in full-color and cut-out books.

Central Plains Book Manufacturing, 22234 C Street, Winfield KS 67156; 877-278-2726; Fax: 316-221-4762. This is a new book printing company that rose out of the ashes of Gilliland Printing.

Commercial Printing Company, 2661 S Pacific Highway, Medford OR 97501; 800-388-7575; Fax: 541-734-7846. Specializes in lay-flat bindings. Can do thick books.

Commonwealth Litho, 310 S Nina Drive #12, Mesa AZ 85210; 480-649-6494; Fax: 480-649-9324. Email: mwpappas1@cox.net. Short run book printers.

Complete Reproduction Service, 411 N Sullivan Street, Santa Ana CA 92703; 714-953-9300; Fax: 714-953-0807.

Corley Printing, 3777 Rider Trail S, Saint Louis MO 63045; 314-739-3777; Fax: 314-739-1436. Email: books@corleyprinting.com. Offices in Atlanta, Chicago, and Kansas City. Specialties: 7 x 10 and 8 1/2 x 11 books, catalogs, and directories. In business since 1929.

Custom Printing Company, 200 Monroe Avenue, Frederick MD 21701; 301-663-1494; 800-553-1494. Also plant at Van Hoffman Graphics, 1005 Commercial Drive, Owensville MO 65066; 573-437-4161; 800-325-8323; Fax: 573-437-2785. Specialists in printing manuals, textbooks, and directories.

Daamen Inc., W Rutland Industrial Park, P O Box 97, West Rutland VT 05777; 802-438-5472; 800-570-5470; Fax: 802-428-5477. Email: daamenprin@aol.com. Book printer only, with a 3 to 4 week schedule. Perfect and saddle binding, spiral and wire-o as well.

Dallas Offset, 2110 Panoramic Circle, P O Box 223664, Dallas TX 75212; 214-630 8741; Fax: 214-638-7796. 60% of their business is in printing books and directories.

Darby Printing, 6215 Purdue Drive, Atlanta GA 30336; 404-344-2665; 800-241-5292; Fax: 404-346-3332. 70% of their business is in printing books and directories.

Data Reproductions, 4545 Glenmeade Lane, Auburn Hills MI 48326; 248-371-3700; 800-242-3114; Fax: 248-371-3701. Email: datarepro@wwnet.net. Since 1967, all bindings, from 500 to 30,000 copies.

Davidson Printing, 4444 Haines Road, Duluth MN 55816; 218-733-2590; 800-777-7609; Fax: 218-733-2603.

DeHart's Printing Services Corporation, 3265 Scott Boulevard, Santa Clara CA 95054; 408-982-9118; 888-982-4763; Fax: 408-982-9912. Email: leads@deharts.com. Offers on-demand and offset printing from 25 to 2,500 copies, one or two-color text. Bindings: perfect, casebound, saddlestitched, wire-o, or spiral.

Des Plaines Publishing, 1000 Executive Way, Des Plaines IL 60018; 847-824-1111; 800-283-1776; Fax: 847-824-1112. 17% of their business is in printing books and directories.

Dickinson Press, Vice President of Sales, 5100 33rd Street SE, Grand Rapids MI 49512; 616-957-5100; Fax: 616-957-1261. Email: sales@dickinsonpress.com. Established in

1884. Prints educational workbooks, non-standard trim sizes (including pocket dictionaries), mini-books, Bibles, and more.

<u>Documation LLC</u>, 1556 International Drive, Eau Claire WI 54701; 715-839-8899; 800-951-6729; Fax: 715-836-7411. They produce books on demand (from one at a time) to runs up to 25,000 copies. They provide perfect binding, plastic coil or wire-o, saddle-stitch, or ring binders.

<u>Dollco Printing</u>, 2340 St. Laurent Boulevard, Ottawa, Ontario K1G 6E3 Canada; 613-738-9181; Fax: 613-738-4655. 15% of their business is in printing books.

<u>Dome Printing & Lithograph</u>, 340 Commerce Circle, P O Box 2054, Sacramento CA 95815; 916-923-3663; 800-343-3139; Fax: 916-923-9310. 30% of their business is in printing books and directories.

<u>R.R. Donnelley & Sons</u>, 77 W Wacker Drive, Chicago IL 60601; 312-326-8000; 800-742-4455; Fax: 312-326-7074. With many plants and offices, Donnelley is the largest printer in the United States.

Dot Graphics, 8714 Darby Avenue, Northridge CA 91325; 818-341-6666; Fax: 818-700-8475. Email: <u>dotgraph@pacbell.net</u>.

<u>EBSCO Media</u>, 801 5th Avenue South, Birmingham AL 35233; 888-398-4413; Fax: 800-756-6742. Email: <u>bweathers@ebsco.com</u>. Specialty: paperback books in about two weeks. Criteria for Book Program Discount Pricing: Format: 4" x 6" to 8 1/2" x 11". Cover: 10 pt. C1S; 4/0 or 4/1; lay flat, gloss film laminate. Text: 50# or 60# offset; 1/1 or 2/2; On disk or camera ready. Binding: Perfect bind,

saddlestitch, or wire-o. Quantities: 1000 to 10,000. They've been printing books and magazines for more than 50 years.

Edwards Brothers, 2500 S State, P O Box 1007, Ann Arbor MI 48106-1007; 734-769-1000; Fax: 734-769-0350.

Fox Integrity Graphics, 1010 Day Hill Road, P O Box 458, Windsor CT 06095; 860-688-5200; Fax: 860-285-8414. 10% of their business is printing books.

Fry Communications, 800 W Church Road, Mechanicsburg PA 17055; 717-766-0211; 800-334-1429; Fax: 717-691-0341. Email: info@frycomm.com. 2% of their business is printing books, 10% printing directories. Higher quantities a specialty.

Gorham Printing, 334 Harris Road, Rochester WA 98579; 800-837-0970; Fax: 360-360-8679. Email: kurtg@gorhamprinting.com. A short-run printer (25 copies to 3,000) catering to small and self-publishers. Also offers design and layout services. They offer a free 64-page book, A Guide to Book Printing and Self-Publishing.

Graphic Arts Center Publishing, 3019 NW Yeon, P O Box 10306, Portland OR 97210; 503-226-2402; 800-452-3032; Fax: 503-223-1410. Specialty: Full-color books in runs under 10,000.

Gray Printing, 401 E North Street, P O Box 840, Fostoria OH 44830; 419-435-6638; 800-837-4729; Fax: 419-435-9410. 25% of their business is in printing books, the rest in printing catalogs and magazines.

Great Lakes Lithograph, 4005 Clark Avenue, Cleveland OH 44109-1186; 216-651-1500; 800-765-4846; Fax: 216-651-8311. 10% of their business is in printing books.

Harold Buchholz Print Services, 1325 White Marlin Lane, Virginia Beach VA 23464; 757-467-0763; Fax: 603-947-9005. Print runs from 50 to 10,000 copies. Quotes on jobs submitted through PrintUSA.com (see below).

HCI Printing, Health Communications, 800-851-9100; Fax: 800-424-7652. Email: terryb@hcibooks.com. This division of Health Communications, publishers of the *Chicken Soup for the Soul* series, prints their own books as well as books from others.

The John Henry Company, 5400 W Grand River Avenue, P O Box 17099, Lansing MI 48901-4906; 517-323-9000; 800-748-0517; Fax: 800-968-5646. A casebound book binder.

Heritage Press, 8939 Premier Row, Dallas TX 75247; 214-637-2700; 800-392-7377; Fax: 214-589-2205. 10% of their business is printing books.

Hignell Book Printing, 488 Burnell Street, Winnipeg, Manitoba R3G 2B4 Canada; 204-784-1030; 800-304-5553; Fax: 204-774-4053. Email: books@hignell.mb.ca. Founded in 1908. Offers great prices, especially with the difference in Canadian and U.S. dollars.

Impressions Unlimited, 2300 Windsor Court #C, Addison IL 60101; 630-705-6464; Fax: 630-705-1598. Email: sales@impressionsunltd.com. Short-run offset and docutech printing. All bindings. Also fulfillment and warehousing.

Inland Book, W141 N9450 Fountain Boulevard, Menomonee Falls WI 53051; 262-255-5800; 800-552-2235; Fax: 252-255-9730. 80% of their business is in printing books.

Instantpublisher.com, P O Box 985, 410 Highway 72 W, Collierville TN 38027; 800-259-2592. They can print from 25 to 5,000 copies straight from your computer in less than seven days. They use digital print from short runs and offset printing for longer runs.

IPC Communications Services, 501 Colonial Drive, Saint Joseph MI 49085; 616-983-7105; Fax: 616-983-9162. 35% of their business is in printing books and directories.

Japs-Olson Company, 7500 Excelsior Boulevard, Saint Louis Park MN 55426-4519; 612-912-9393; 800-548-2897; Fax: 612-912-1900. Founded in 1907, this company prints books, magazines, catalogs, and direct mail packages. They operate the world's first 12-color sheetfed press.

Johnson Printing, 1880 South 57th Court, Boulder CO 80301; 303-443-1576; Fax: 303-443-1679. 30% of its business is in printing books and directories.

Jostens Commercial Publications, 401 Science Park Road, State College PA 16803; 570-752-9492; 800-322-9725; 570-752-9493. This yearbook printer with plants around the country also prints books for publishers.

Kirby Litho, 2900 S Eads Street, Arlington VA 22202-4011; 703-684-7600; 800-932-3594; Fax: 703-683-5918. Email: bkt@kirby-litho.com. Founded in 1927, 75% of their business is in printing books and directories.

King Printing, 181 Industrial Avenue, Lowell MA 01852; 978-458-2345, ext. 129; Fax: 978-458-3026. Email: chughson@kingprinting.com. King offers short run on-demand books from 1 to 25,000. Binding includes case binding, perfect, lay-flat perfect, wire O, saddle, and glue. Applications include galleys, custom courseware textbooks, high-tech manuals, journals. King is a certified minority-owned company. Credit cards accepted.

Kni, Inc., 1261 S State College Parkway, Anaheim CA 92806; 800-886-7301. Email: knimb@aol.com. Founded in 1972.

C.J. Krehbiel Company, 3962 Virginia Avenue, Cincinnati OH 45227; 513-271-6035; 800-598-7808; Fax: 513-271-6082. Since 1872. Email: rickh@cjkrehbiel.com.

Lake Book Manufacturing, 2085 N Cornell Avenue, Melrose Park IL 60160; 708-345-7000; Fax: 708-345-1544.

The Lehigh Press, 51 Haddonfield Road, Cherry Hill NJ 08002; 609-665-5200; Fax: 609-665-0323. Specializes in digital prepress, direct market printing, and book components and specialities.

Lewis Creative Technologies, 900 W Leigh Street, P O Box 27122, Richmond VA 23261; 804-648-4448; Fax: 804-644-3502. 30% of their business is in printing books. Short-run only.

Lithocolor Press, 9825 W Roosevelt Road, Westchester IL 60154; 708-345-5530; Fax: 708-345-1283. Paperback book specialist: sheetfed or web, saddlestitch or perfect-bound.

Lithoid Printing, 19 Cotters Lane, East Brunswick NJ 08816; 732-238-4000; Fax: 732-238-9628. Web and sheetfed printers of softcover books in press runs from 1,000 to 50,000 since 1951.

Malloy Incorporated, Bill Upton, President, 5411 Jackson Road, P O Box 1124, Ann Arbor MI 48106-1124; 734-665-6113; 800-722-3231; Fax: 734-665-2326. Email: custservice@malloy.com. Also has sales offices in Illinois, California, Washington, and New York. They publish a quarterly newsletter, the *Malloy Quarterly*. They offer RepKover lay-flat binding, bind-in CD-ROMs, precision spot gloss, and more.

Maple-Vail Book Manufacturing Group, Main Office, Willow Springs Lane, P O Box 2695, York PA 17405; 717-764-5911; Fax: 717-764-4702. Southeastern Sales Office, 1441 Wiley Oakley Drive, P O Box 1064, Gatlinburg TN 37738; 423-430-5900; Fax: 423-436-0420. Email: donnelly@maple-vail.com.

Maracle Press, 1156 King Street E, P O Box 606, Oshawa, Ontario L1H 7N4; 800-558-8604; Fax: 905-428-6024. Email: maracle@maraclepress.com. 50% of their business is in printing books and directories.

Marathon Printing, 9 N Third Street, Philadelphia PA 19106; 215-238-1100; Fax: 215-625-0339. 10% of their business is in printing books and directories.

Marrakech Express, 720 Wesley Avenue, Tarpon Springs FL 34689; 727-942-2218; 800-940-6566; Fax: 727-937-4758. Email: print@marrak.com. Prints books, journals, magazines, and newsletters.

Maverick Publications, P O Box 5007 (97708), 63324 Nels Anderson Road, Bend OR 97701; 541-382-6978; 800-800-4831; Fax: 541-382-4831. Email: gmasher@mavbooks.com. They do short runs.

McNaughton & Gunn, 960 Woodland Drive, P O Box 10, Saline MI 48176-0010; 734-429-8712; Fax: 800-677-BOOK. Also sales offices in New York, North Carolina, Illinois, and California.

Millennia Graphics, 1225 Aeroplaza Drive, Colorado Springs CO 80916; 719-638-0991, ext. 11; Fax: 719-638-0992. Email: rlkuckuck@milleniagraphics.com. Their standard schedule for perfect-bound books is 10 days, casebound books in four weeks. 6x9 and 7x10 are their most efficient sizes.

Moran Printing, 5425 Florida Boulevard, Baton Rouge LA 70806; 800-211-8335. Book printer since 1880.

Morgan Printing, 900 Old Koenig Lane #135, Austin TX 78756; 512-459-5194; 800-421-5593; Fax: 512-451-0755. Email: morganp@flash.net. Specialty: 100 to 3,000 copies.

Morris Publishing, 3212 E Highway 30, Kearney NE 68847; 800-650-7888. For cookbook self-publishers.

Muscle Bound Bindery, 701 Plymouth Avenue N, Minneapolis MN 55411; 612-522-4406; Fax: 612-522-0927. Bindery only, primarily casebound.

National Publishing, 11311 Roosevelt Boulevard, P O Box 16234, Philadelphia PA 19154; 215-676-1863; 800-570-7235; Fax: 215-856-9930. This division of the Courier Corporation prints books, especially Bibles and other high page count books requiring special papers.

NetPub Corporation, 2 Neptune Road, Poughkeepsie NY 12601; 845-463-1100; 800-724-1100; Fax: 845-463-0018. Email: wgrogg@netpub.net. Email: jdickson@netpub.net. "We are an on-demand digital printing company who specializes in the short-run (1 to 2,000 copies) printing of books, tutorials, manuals, reports, and collateral print materials.

Network Printers, Bill Papke, 1010 South 70th Street, Milwaukee WI 53214-31033; 414-443-0530; Fax: 414-443-0536. Email: info@network-printers.com. Print runs from 250 to 5,000 copies.

Odyssey Press, 113 Crosby Road #15, Dover NH 03820; 603-749-4433; Fax: 603-749-1425. 30% of their business is in printing books.

Offset Paperback Manufacturers, P O Box N (Route 309), Dallas PA 18612; 570-673-5261; Fax: 570-675-8714. A division of Bertlesman, this company specializes in softcover books, both trade and mass market.

One 2 One Direct, 27460 Avenue Scott, Valencia CA 91355; 661-294-9000; 866-220-0121; Fax: 661-702-9001. Email: bill.frank@121Direct.net. Provides short-run book printing, from 200 to 2,000 copies, with any amount of page counts. From digital file or camera-ready copy. Saddlestitch, perfect binding, and accubind. Also storage and fulfillment.

Optic Graphics, 101 Dover Road, Glen Burnie MD 21060; 410-768-3000; 800-638-7107; Fax: 410-760-4082.

Oregon Lithoprint, 611 E Third, P O Box 727, McMinnville OR 97128; 800-472-1198; Fax: 503-434-1462. 20% of their business is in printing books and directories.

Overseas Printing Corporation, 99 The Embarcadero, San Francisco CA 94105; 415-835-9999; Fax: 415-835-9899. Email: hal@overseasprinting.com.

Pacific Rim International Printing, 11726 San Vicente Boulevard #280, Los Angeles CA 90049; 800-95-COLOR; Fax: 310-207-2566. Email: lorid@pacrim-intl.com. Since 1987, they are full service manufacturers of books, catalogs, calendars, and brochures (working with Hong Kong partners and affiliate companies).

Paper Expert, Resource for book, catalog and magazine publishers. You can save money and improve efficiency through a tailored Paper Program. Extensive paper and printing related links and resources on site as well.

Patterson Printing, 1550 Territorial Road, Benton Harbor MI 49022; 616-925-2177; 800-848-8826; Fax: 616-925-6057. Email: sales@patterson-printing.com. Founded in 1956.

Pease Bindery, 111 Oakcreek Drive, Lincoln NE 68528; 402-476-1303; Fax: 402-476-3978. Book binders. Also loose leaf products.

Phoenix Color, 540 Western Maryland Parkway, Hagerstown MD 21740; 800-632-4111; Fax: 301-791-9560. Email: jruggeri@phoenixcolor.com. They specialize in printing jackets, book covers, and other components, especially with special effects, die cuts, etc. They now also print books. Their Thin Book Division (ext. 3200) in New Jersey produces high quality multicolor soft and hardcover thin books. Their Book Technology Park division (ext. 5099) in Maryland manufactures one- and two-color offset books in soft or hardcover. They also offer print-on-demand capability.

Sterling Pierce Company, 422 Atlantic Avenue, East Rockaway NY 11518; 516-593-1170; Fax: 516-593-1401. Galley copies a specialty.

Pinnacle Press, 2662 Metro Boulevard, Saint Louis MO 63043; 314-291-2230; Fax: 314-291-8842. Email: tom@pinnaclepress.com. Printer and finisher of 4-color dust jackets, paperback covers, etc.

The Press of Ohio, 3765 Sunnybrook Road, Brimfield OH 44240; 330-678-5868; Fax: 330-677-8256. 50% of their business is printing books.

Prinit Press, 211 NW 7th Street, Richmond VA 47374; 765-966-7130; 800-478-4885; Fax: 765-966-7131. A division of AP Group.

Publishers' Graphics, 1100 Elm Hill Pike, Nashville TN 37210; 888-321-0540; Fax: 615-256-3089 or Kathleen Perkins, 1701 Quincy Avenue, Naperville IL 60540; 888-404-3769. Founded in 1996. Short-run printing in quantities from 1 to 2,000. Casebound, perfect-bound, or mechanical bindings. They also print digital color in-house.

Quebecor World, 340 Pemberwick Road, Greenwich CT 06831; 203-532-4200; 800-678-6299; Fax: 203-532-3425. Email: contact.bookservices@quebecorworld.com. Corporate headquarters: 612 St. Jacques, Montreal, QC Canada H36 4M8; 514-954-0101; Fax: 514-954-3624. One of the largest printers in North America, it has several divisions that print mass market and trade books.

Quinn Woodbine, 419 Park Avenue South #1201, New York NY 10016; 212-889-0552; Fax: 212-679-8156.

V G Reed & Sons, 1002 South 12th Street, Louisville KY 40210; 502-589-3770; 800-635-9788; Fax: 502-589-9010. 20% of their business is in printing books and directories.

Reindl Bindery Co., 111 E Reindl Way, Glendale WI 53212; 414-906-1111; 800-878-1121; Fax: 414-906-1110. Email: info@reindlbindery.com. A full-service trade bindery.

The John Roberts Co., 9687 E River Road, Minneapolis MN 55433; 612-755-5500; Fax: 612-755-0394. Prints some books and booklets, but only in 25,000 on up quantities.

Rose Printing, 2503 Jackson Bluff Road (32304), P O Box 5078, Tallahassee FL 32314; 850-576-4151; 800-227-3725; Fax: 850-576-4153. Email: charlesr@roseprinting.com. Prints short-run books, catalogs, and booklets. Offers RepKover lay-flat binding. Can do books of all sizes, with a specialty in mini-books.

St. Joseph Printing, 50 Macintosh Boulevard, Concord, Ontario L4K 4P3 Canada; 905-660-3111; 888-654-4980; Book Fax: 905-660-9737; Fax: 905-660-6820. Email: info@stjoseph.com. U.S. address: Rob Cruz, Account Executive, 90 Raynor Avenue, Ronkonkoma NY 11779; 516-588-3434; Fax: 516-588-7583. Web and sheetfed offset printing of catalogs, magazines, books, and other materials. Saddlestitch and perfect binding.

Sentinel Printing Company, 8525 Edinbrook Crossing #107-E, Brooklyn Park MN 55443; 763-488-9960; Fax: 763-488-9961. Email: sperillo@sentinelprinting.com. Printing plant: 250 N Highway 10, Saint Cloud MN 56304; 320-251-6434; 800-450-6434; Fax: 320-251-6273. Printing books, catalogs, directories, and manuals since 1854. Print runs from 500 to millions. Bindings: saddlestitch, perfect, and plastic-coil.

Sheridan Books, 613 E Industrial Drive, Chelsea MI 48118; 734-475-9145; 800-999-2665; Fax: 734-475-7337. Email: jstirling@sheridanbooks.com. Formed in 1999 when the parent company of Braun-Brumfield bought BookCrafters. The Sheriden Group also owns United Litho and the Sheridan Press.

ShortRunBooks.com, 215 East 3rd Street, Des Moines IA 50309; 800-798-3278; Fax: 515-288-4210. Email: Shortrunbooks@dilleymfg.com. A division of Dilley Manufacturing, this company can print and bind short runs. Specialty: Binder-based books and reports.

Signature Book Printing, 8041 Cessna Avenue #132, Gaithersburg MD 20879; 301-258-8353; Fax: 301-670-4147. Email: book@worldweb.net.

The Stinehour Press, 853 Lancaster Road, Lunenburg VT 05906; 802-328-2507; 800-331-7753; Fax: 802-328-3960. Email: stevestinehour@stinehourpress.com. Motto: Complete book printing services for scholarly and cultural institutions, and all publishers of specialized books. One of the few still offering letterpress printing. Also warehousing and shipping services. Also offers design services. They print some gorgeous books.

TAN Books & Publishers, 2119 North Central Avenue, Rockford IL 61103; 815-987-1831; Fax: 815-987-1833.

TCS, 110 West 12th Avenue, North Kansas City MO 64116; 816-842-9770; Fax: 816-842-0628. Email: dteeters@tcsbook.com. Perfect-bound, saddlestitched, plastic coil; turn time is less than 15 days from receipt of copy or disk.

Thomson-Shore, 7300 W Joy Road, Dexter MI 48130-9701; 734-426-3939; Fax: 734-426-6216; Fax: 800-706-4545. Founded in 1972. An employee-owned printer of books, from 200 to 20,000 copies. Ask for a copy of their *Printer's Ink* newsletter.

Total Printing Systems, 103 E Morgan, Newton IL 62448; 618-783-2978; 800-465-5200; Fax: 618-783-8407. Short run book and booklet (up to 100,000 copies) printing with perfect, saddle, 3-ring, wire-o, and loose-leaf bindings.

Transcontinental Printing Book Group, 1201, rue Marie-Victorin, Saint-Bruno-de-Montarville, Quebec J3V 6C3 Canada; 450-441-1201; 800-361-3699 (US and Canada); Fax: 450-441-4242. Email: beaudind@transcontinental.ca. Founded in 1975, Transcontinental consists of five printers in Canada (Interglobe Printing, Métropole Litho, Métrolitho, Imprimerie Gagné, and Best Book Manufacturers). Books contribute about $100 million of their $818 million in annual business.

Tri-State Graphics, 500 Iowa Street, Dubuque IA 52001; 319-556-8430; Fax: 319-556-6313. Email: ksohl@tsgd.com. Short run printing, digital and offset, with perfect-binding, saddlestitiching, and plastic coil.

Tri-State Litho, 71-81 TenBroeck Avenue, Kingston NY 12401; 845-331-7581; 800-836-7581; Fax: 845-331-1571. Email: tristate@ulster.net.

Unimac Graphics, 340 Michele Place, Carlstadt NJ 07072; 201-372-9650; Fax: 201-372-0699. 20% of their business is in printing books.

United Book Press, 1807 Whitehead Road, Baltimore MD 21207; 410-944-4044; 800-726-0120; Fax: 410-944-4049. Email: Unitedbook@aol.com. Two week delivery on paperbound books, 4 weeks for casebound. Since 1989.

United Graphics Inc., 2916 Marshall Avenue, P O Box 559, Mattoon IL 61938; 217-235-7161; Fax: 217-234-6274. An employee-owned printer of books, catalogs, journals, and directories.

United Graphics Inc., 642 Parkview Road, Terre Haute IN 47803; 812-232-0478; Fax: 812-232-4048. Email: info@bookmanufacturer.com.

Van Volumes, P O Box 449, Palmer MA 01069; 413-283-8556; Fax: 413-283-7884. Email: vanvol@samnet.net.

Vaughan Printing, 411 Cowan Street, Nashville TN 37207; 615-256-2244; Fax: 615-259-4576. Email: bookprint@aol.com.

Versa Press, 1465 Spring Bay Road, P O Box 2460, East Peoria IL 61611; 309-822-8272; 800-447-7829; Fax: 309-822-8141.

Victor Graphics, 1211 Bernard Drive, Baltimore MD 21223; 410-233-8300; 800-899-8303; Fax: 410-233-8304. Email: pineapple@victorgraphics.com. Founded in 1983. Sales offices in New York, Illinois, Maryland, Massachusetts, Georgia, Ohio, and California.

<u>Von Hoffman Graphics</u>, 1000 Camera Avenue, Saint Louis MO 63126; 314-966-0909; Fax: 314-966-0983. Eldridge Facility: 400 South 14th Avenue, Eldridge IA 52748; 800-422-9336. Frederick Facility: 200 Monroe Avenue, Frederick MD 21701; 800-553-1494. Owensville Facility: 1005 Commercial Drive, Owensville MO 65066; 573-437-4161; 800-325-8323; Fax: 573-437-2785. 50% of their business is printing books, 1- and 2-color. Their Von Hoffman Press division is devoted exclusively to the educational market. Their Von Hoffman Graphics division offers one- and two-color printing for both educational and commercial book markets. They also print catalogs, inserts, and manuals. Their Precision Offset division specializes in lithographic printing of plastics (including overhead transparencies, plastic textbook inserts, static clings, etc.

<u>Walsworth Publishing</u>, 306 N Kansas Avenue, Marceline MO 64658; 660-376-3543; 800-369-2646; Fax: 660-258-7798.

<u>Webcom</u>, 3480 Pharmacy Avenue, Toronto, Ontario M1W 2S7 Canada; 416-496-1000; 800-665-9322; Fax: 416-496-1537. Full service book manufacturer with complete in-house production, long-run web and short-run digital print as well as electronic publishing products.

<u>Webcrafters</u>, P O Box 7608 (53707), 2211 Fordem Avenue, Madison WI 53704; 608-244-3561; 800-356-8200; Fax: 608-244-5120. Email: <u>info@webcrafters-inc.com</u>. Sales offices in Connecticut, Florida, California, New Jersey, Massachusetts, Illinois, and Madison. Second plant at 5487 N Blue Bill Park Drive, Westport WI 53597. Bindings: saddlestitch, spiral, perfectbinding, and Wire-O. Can also do kitting and special packaging.

Whitehall Printing, 4244 Corporate Square, Naples FL 34104-4753; 941-643-6464; 800-321-9290; Fax: 941-643-6439. Email: johng@whitehallprinting.com. Call for their standard pricing sheets. Among the lowest-cost printers in the U.S. since 1959.

Worzalla Publishing Company, 3535 Jefferson Street, Stevens Point WI 54481; 715-344-9600; 800-442-2463; Fax: 715-344-2578. Specializes in short runs of full-color books, especially children's books. Since 1892.

A List of Book Distributors

Advantage Publ. Group
5880 Oberlin Dr., Ste. 400
San Diego, CA 92121-4735
(858) 450-3598 phone
(800) 499-3822 fax
shaunaa@advmkt.com
www.advantagebooksonline.com

Alliance House Dist.
220 Ferris Ave., Ste. 201
White Plains, NY 10603-3462
(914) 328-5456 phone
(914) 946-1929 fax
alliancehs@aol.com

American West Books
1831 Industrial Way #101
Sanger, CA. 93657
(559) 876-2170
Fax: (559) 876-2180

Antique Collectors Club
91 Market Street , Industrial Park
Wappingers Falls, NY 12590
(914) 297-0003 phone
(914) 297-0068 fax
info@antiquecc.com
www.antiquecc.com

Authorlink!
3720 Millswood Drive
Irving, TX 75062
(972) 650-1986 phone
(972) 650-1622 fax
dbooth@authorlink.com
www.authorlink.com

Biblio Distribution
4720 Boston Way
Lanham, MD 20706
(301) 459-3366 phone
(301) 459-1705 fax
dfullerton@bibliodistribution.com
www.bibliodistribution.com

Book Clearing House
46 Purdy Street
Harrison House, NY 10528
(800) 431-1579 phone
(914) 835-0015 fax
smallpressbch@aol.com
www.bookch.com

BookMasters Inc.
30 Amberwood Parkway
Ashland, OH 44805
(800) 537-6727 phone
dwurster@bookmaster.com
www.bookmaster.com

BookWorld Services, Inc.
1933 Whitfield Park Look
Sarasota, FL 34243-4093
(941) 758-8094 phone
(941) 753-9396 fax
info@bookworld.com
www.bookworld.com

Canbook Distribution Services

1220 Nicholson Rd.
NewMarket, Ontario L3Y 7V1
(905) 836-5807 phone
(905) 363-2665 fax
inquiry@canbook.com
www.canbook.com

CDS/BookWorld

Attn Christian Product Division
1933 Whitfield Park Loop
Sarasota, FL 34243
(800) 905-4603 Ext. 250 phone
(800) 777-2525 fax
info@bookworld.com
www.bookworld.com

Charles E. Tuttle Co., Inc.

1 Box 231-5
North Clarenden, VT 05759
(802) 773-8930 phone
(800) 329-8885 fax
info@tuttlepublishing.com
www.tuttlepublishing.com

Client Distribution Services

425 Madison Ave., Ste. 1500
New York, NY 10017
(212) 223-2969
(212) 223-1504

Combined Publishing (Military)

1024 Fayette Street
Conshohocken, PA 19428-0307
(610) 828-2595 phone
(610) 828-2603 fax
combined@combinedpublishing.com
www.combinedpublishing.com

Consortium Book Sales

1045 Westgate Drive, Ste. 90
St. Paul, MN 55114-1065
(612) 221-9035 phone
(612) 221-0124 fax
consortium@cbsd.com
www.cbsd.com

Distributed Art Publ.

155 6th Ave., 2nd Floor
New York, NY 10013-1507
(212) 627-1999 phone
(212) 627-9484 fax

FaithWorks

Mr. Larry Carpenter
9247 Hunterboro Drive
Brentwood, TN 37027
(615) 221-6442 phone
(615) 221-6442 fax
lcarpenter@faithworksonline.com
www.faithworksonline.com

Greenleaf Book Group LLC
660 Elmwood Point
Aurora, OH 44202
(800) 932-5420 phone
(330) 995-9704 fax
client@greenleafbookgroup.com
www.greenleafbookgroup.com

Independent Publishers Group
814 N. Franklin Street
Chicago, IL 60610-3109
(312) 337-0747 phone
(312) 337-5985 fax
frontdesk@ipgbook.com
www.ipgbook.com

International Publishers Marketing
22841 Quicksilver Drive
Sterling, VA 20166
(703) 661-1586 phone
(703) 661-1501 fax
ipmcomments@booksintl.com
www.internationalpubmarket.com

IUniverse.com
5220 S. 16th Street, Ste. 200
Lincoln, NE 68512
(800) 376-1736 phone
(402) 323-7824 fax
pubservices@iuniverse.com
www.iuniverse.com

LPC Group
1436 W. Randolph Street
Chicago, IL 60607-1414
(800) 243-0138 phone
(800) 334-3892 fax
lpc-info@lpcgroup.com
www.lpcgroup.com

Midpoint Trade Books Inc.
27 W. 20th Street
New York, N.Y. 10011-3707
(212) 727-0190 phone
(212) 727-0195 fax
midpointny@aol.com
www.midpointtrade.com

National Book Network
4720 Boston Way
Lanham, MD 20706
(301) 459-3366 phone
(301) 459-1705 fax
contact vehicle on website
www.nbnbooks.com

Origin Book Sales
2961 California Ave., Ste. E
Salt Lake City, UT 84104-4581
(801) 872-8060 phone
(801) 972-6570 fax
info@originbook.com
www.originbook.com

Partners Publishers Group
2325 Jarco Drive
Holt, MI 44842
(517) 694-3205 phone
(517) 694-0617 fax
partnerss@aol.com

Penton Overseas, Inc.
2470 Impala Drive
Carlsbad, CA 92008-7226
(760) 431-0060 phone
(760) 431-8110 fax
info@pentonoverseas.com
www.pentonoverseas.com

Publishers Group West
1700 Fourth Street
Berkeley, CA 94710
(510) 528-1444 phone
(510) 528-3444 fax
info@pgw.com
www.pgw.com

Samuel Weiser Inc.
P.O. Box 612
York Beach, ME 03910
(207) 363-4393 phone
(207) 363-5799 fax
email@weiserbooks.com
www.weiserbooks.com

SCB Distributors
15608 S. New Century Drive
Gardens, CA 90248
(310) 532-9400 phone
(310) 532-7001 fax
scb@scbdistributors.com
www.scbdistributors.com

Seven Hills Book Dist.
2961531 Tremont St.
Cincinnati, OH 45214
(513) 381-3881 phone
(513) 381-0753 fax
customerservice@sevenhillsbook
s.com
www.sevenhillsbooks.com

Sunbelt Publications
1250 Fayette Street
El Cajon, CA. 92020-1511
(619) 258-4911
(619) 258-4916 fax

Wimmer Cookbook, R.R.
4210 BG Goodrich Blvd.
Memphis, TN 38118
(901) 362-8900 phone
(901) 346-9918 fax

Words Distributing Co.
7900 Edgewater Drive
Oakland, CA 94621-2004
(510) 553-9673 phone
(510) 553-0729 fax
words@wordsdistributing.com
www.wordsdistributing.com

Online Resources

American National Standards Institute (ANSI)
The ANSI Federation's primary goal is the enhancement of global competitiveness of U.S. business and the American quality of life by promoting and facilitating voluntary consensus standards and conformity assessment systems and promoting their integrity. The Institute represents the interests of its nearly 1,400 company, organization, government agency, institutional and international members. ANSI does not itself develop American National Standards (ANSs); rather it facilitates development by establishing consensus among qualified groups.
http://www.ansi.org

Book Industry Systems Advisory Committee (BISAC)
BISAC, the Book Industry Systems Advisory Committee started up as a result of a meeting to promote the use of the ISBN. BISAC has been a Committee of the Book Industry Study Group since 1980. (See BASIC below)
http://www.bisg.org/basic.html

Book And Serial Industry Communications (BASIC)
BISAC, the Book Industry Systems Advisory Committee began as a result of a meeting to promote the use of the ISBN in the publishing industry. The other group evolving at the same time was SISAC, the Serials Industry Systems Advisory Committee, to do similar work for the ISSN. These two committees have combined into one organization, BASIC, which continues to carry out the work of both BISAC and SISAC, and to provide accurate and current research information about the industry.
http://www.bisg.org/basic.html

Cataloging in Publication (CIP)
The purpose of the Cataloging in Publication (CIP) program is to prepare prepublication cataloging records for those books most likely to be widely acquired by the nation's libraries. For further information about the CIP program and how your publishing house may apply for participation in the program, write to:
Library of Congress, Cataloging in Publication Division, COLL/CIP (4320) Washington, DC 20450-4320.

International Organization for Standardization (ISO)

The International Organization for Standardization (ISO) is a worldwide federation of national standards bodies from some 100 countries, one from each country. The mission of ISO is to promote the development of standardization and related activities in the world with a view to facilitating the international exchange of goods and services, and to developing cooperation in the spheres of intellectual, scientific, technological and economic activity. ISO's work results in international agreements which are published as International Standards.
http://www.iso.ch

International Standard Serial Number (ISSN)

The International Standard Serial Number (ISSN) is a code used on catalogues, databases or commercial transactions each time serial publications are involved. In order to fulfil its goal in an efficient way, the ISSN, as any standardized international code, must be universally used. It is thus available for all partners concerned, at each stage of the information chain.
http://www.issn.org

Library of Congress (LC)

The Library of Congress' mission is to make its resources available and useful to the Congress and the American people and to sustain and preserve a universal collection of knowledge and creativity for future generations. The Library serves as the research arm of Congress and is recognized as the national library of the United States. Its collections comprise the world's most comprehensive record of human creativity and knowledge. Open to those above high school age without charge or special permission, it is the world's largest library and a great resource to scholars and researchers.
http://lcweb.loc.gov

Library of Congress Control Number (LCCN)

The Library of Congress Control Number or LCCN is a number assigned by the Library of Congress to an individual bibliographic item.
http://www.fsc.follett.com/products/marctags/tag010.cfm

National Information Standards Organization (NISO)
The National Information Standards Organization (NISO)is a nonprofit
association accredited as a standards developer by the American
National Standards Institute, the national clearinghouse for voluntary
standards development in the U.S. NISO is a leader in shaping
international standards. The goal in using technical standards in
information services, libraries, and publishing is to achieve compatibility
and therefore interoperability between equipment, data, practices, and
procedures in order to make information services more productive.
http://www.niso.org

PubEasy.com
PubEasy.com is an Internet inquiry and ordering service for the global
bookselling industry. Booksellers from almost 100 countries use this
service daily to access title, price and availability information, to place
orders, check order status, and to access catalogs from participating
publishers, distributors and wholesalers, twenty-four hours a day, seven
days a week.
http://www.pubeasy.com

PUBNET
PUBNET, the Electronic Commerce division of AAP, provides electronic
data interchange service (EDI) to over 90 publishers representing
hundreds of subsidiaries and imprints. Over 3,700 bookstores, libraries,
wholesalers, and schools are now buying books electronically through
PUBNET®, making it the largest EDI trading community of booksellers
and publishers in the world. PUBNET® also maintains a high-quality
title database of over 340,000 titles from PUBNET® publishers. This
database, specifically designed for the higher education market, is
linked to the ordering system to facilitate the fulfillment process and can
also be accessed separately as a product information source.
http://www.pubnet.org

United States Copyright Office (USCO)
United States Copyright Office (USCO) is an organization "to promote
the progress of science and useful arts, by securing for limited times to
authors and inventors the exclusive right to their respective writings
and discoveries" (U.S. Constitution, Article I, Section 8)
http://lcweb.loc.gov/copyright

X*NET - Evangelical Christian Publishers Association (EPCA)
X.NET was created by the Evangelical Christian and Protestant Church-Owned Publishers Association/Christian Booksellers Association/Gospel Music Association to provide electronic data interchange service (EDI) to publishers within the Christian community. X.NET results in faster turn-around, improved accuracy and lower operating costs for Christian publishing, music, gifts, and other aspects of the industry.
http://www.ecpa.org

Books In Print
This is the Web's premier bibliographic resource! Turn to booksinprint.com for comprehensive, unbiased information on over 3.5 million titles with over 600,000 full-text reviews, 7,000 author bios, 300 book, video and audio awards, stock availability from over 20 major suppliers.

Book Clubs

Anglican Book Club
4000 Massachusetts Ave NW
Suite 1130
Washington, DC 20016
202-244-4443
202-244-5005 fax
Of special interest to
Episcopalians and the worldwide Anglican communion:
art and art history, biography,
theology, spirituality, and
anthologies.

Antiques and Collectibles
Book Club
101 Park Ave.
New York, N.Y. 10178
www.booksonline.com
Books for professional and
serious collectors of antiques.

Arrow Book Club
555 Broadway
New York, NY 10012
212-343-6100
212-505-3217 fax
Paperbound reprints and
originals for grades 4-6.

Book of the Month Club
Time & Life Building
1271 Avenue of the Americas
New York, NY 10020-1393
212-522-4200
212-522-7145 fax

Prevention Book Club
33 E. Minor St.
Emmaus, PA 18049
610-967-5171
Natural health care, nutrition
And natural cooking.

Primary Teachers
Book Club
101 Park Ave.
New York, NY 10178
212-455-5000
212-455-5002 fax
Practical ideas and
activity books for
teachers of grades K-3.

Psychotherapy
Book Club
230 Livingston St.
Northvale, NJ 07647
201-767-4093
201-767-4330 fax
Books for mental health
professionals, behavorial
sciences, human relations,
psychology and psychiatry.

Science Fiction
Book Club
1540 Broadway 16th fl.
New York, NY 10036
212-782-7278
212-782-7210
www.sfbc.com

Book Reviewers

The Midwest Book Review gives priority consideration to small publishers, self-published authors, academic presses, and specialty publishers. To submit a book for review, send:
1. A finished copy of the book (no galleys or uncorrected proofs.
2. An accompanying publicity release or media kit.

James A. Cox, Editor-in-Chief, of Midwest Book Review, says there is a 12 to 16-week "window of opportunity" for a book to be assigned out for review. If a book makes the cut and is featured, Midwest Book Review will automatically send a tear sheet to the publisher.

Send submissions to: James A. Cox, Editor-in-Chief, Midwest Book Review, 278 Orchard Drive
Oregon, WI 53575

Elizabeth Routen
Critique Magazine
critique@windriverpress.com
http://routen.windriverpress.com
Categories: Art, Australian Books, Computer/Internet/Technology, Books From Small Presses, Features, Fiction, General, Humanities, Literature, Non-Fiction, Poetry, Biography, eBooks, Writing, promotion & publishing, Science, History/Political, Adventure

Apryl Duncan
FictionAddiction.NET
Box 876
Chattanooga, TN 37343
ReviewRequest@FictionAddiction.NET
http://www.FictionAddiction.NET
Categories: Books From Small Presses, Children's Book, Fiction, Literature, Mystery, Romance, Sci-Fi/Fantasy,

Young Adult/Children's, Thriller/Suspense, Writing, promotion & publishing, Adventure, Horror

Sarah Nesbeitt, Coordinating Editor (USA)
Historical Novels Review
Booth Library, Reference Services
Eastern Illinois University
Charleston, IL 61920
Phone: 217-581-7538
cfsln@eiu.edu
http://www.historicalnovelsociety.org
Categories: Australian Books, Books From Small Presses, Christian, Fiction, Mystery, Romance, Sci-Fi/Fantasy, Thriller/Suspense, Adventure
Comments: Historical fiction (pre-1950s setting) and its associated subgenres: historical mystery, fantasy, religious fiction, and romance IF history plays a strong role in story. No e-books. Please query first w/ title, author, and brief description.

Rachel A Hyde
http://www.myshelf.com
2 Meadow Close
Budleigh Salterton, Devon EX9 6JN
rachelahyde@ntlworld.com
http://www.myshelf,com
Categories: Books From Small Presses, Fiction, Literature, Mystery, Romance, Sci-Fi/Fantasy, Thriller/Suspense, Adventure, Horror
Comments: I review most fiction but especially historicals, romance, historical crime (my speciality), SF, fantasy & romance.

Detra Fitch
Huntress Book Reviews
205 Dana Drive
Easley, SC 29642
huntress@huntressreviews.com
http://www.huntressreviews.com
Categories: Children's Book, Fiction, General, Romance, Sci-Fi/Fantasy, Young Adult/Children's, Thriller/Suspense, Adventure, Horror
Comments: Reviews all types of print and electronic books, EXCEPT non-fiction. She posts the reviews on her site and even sends copys to Barnes & Noble and Amazon.com!

Bill Kent
Kirkus, NYT, WashPostBookWorld
131 Overbrook Parkway
Wynnewood, PA 19096
Phone: 610-642-0484
BKNT@aol.com
Categories: Art, Books From Small Presses, Fiction, Humanities, Literature, Metaphysical, Mystery, Non-Fiction, Pop Culture, Religion, Sci-Fi/Fantasy, Sociology, Spiritual, Travel/Hospitality, Psychology/Mental Health, Biography, Thriller/Suspense, Theater, Politics, Writing, promotion & publishing, Science, History/Political, Adventure, Nature, Horror
Comments: I also contribute to a monthly newsletter for senior citizens published by the Philadelphia Corporation for the Aging interested in books for, by or about people over 55. You may send press releases and info. Do not send books until requested.

John Wallace
Literary Luminaries
P.O. Box 7932
Ocean Beach, CA 92167
john@literaryluminaries.com
http://literaryluminaries.com
Categories: Fiction, Food, General, Literature, Pop Culture,
Religion, Biography, Politics, Film History, History/Political,
Adventure

Charles McCool
LowerAirfares.com
P.O. Box 2755
Reston, VA 20195-0755
Phone: 703-264-9763
admin@lowerairfares.com
http://www.LowerAirfares.com
Categories: Books From Small Presses, Travel/Hospitality,
Adventure
Comments: LowerAirfares.com reviews all books
appropriate for its readers--people that want to save money,
stress, and time on travel. E-mail for street address (if
sending books via non-USPS).

Norman P. Goldman
montrealtravels.com
5567 Alpine
Montreal, Quebec H4V2X4
l.goldman@sympatico.ca
http://www.montrealtavels.com
Categories: Computer/Internet/Technology, Books From
Small Presses, Fiction, Non-Fiction, Travel/Hospitality,
Financial, Business, Adventure, Judaica
Comments: I am an official book reviewer for the
CANADIAN BOOK REVIEW ANNUAL
(http://www.interlog.com/~cbra/) I also published several

book reviews that have appeared on the following web sites. www.bookideas.com http://www.bootsnall.com/cgi-bin/gt/reviews/index

Rebecca Brown
RebeccasReads.com
P. O. Box 371
Clallam Bay, WA 98326-0371
Phone: 360-963-3112
the.editor@rebeccasreads.com
http://www.rebeccasreads.com
Categories: Art, Books From Small Presses, Children's Book, Fiction, General, Health, How-To, Humanities, Library, Literature, Mystery, Non-Fiction, Religion, Sci-Fi/Fantasy, Sociology, Spiritual, Travel/Hospitality, Women, Psychology/Mental Health, Biography, Parenting, Thriller/Suspense, Politics, Self-help, Writing, promotion & publishing, Inspirational/Motivational, Gardening, Science, Education, History/Political, Adventure, Nature, Photography
Comments: Go to http://www.rebeccasreads.com/admin/authsubmn.html for submission details. RebeccasReads reviews 4+ books per week.

Jessica Holmes
Romance At Its Best, Midnight Reviews
owner@romanceatitsbest.com
http://www.romanceatitsbest.com/
Categories: Books From Small Presses, Fiction, General, How-To, Literature, Mystery, Non-Fiction, Romance, Sci-Fi/Fantasy, Women, Young Adult/Children's, Biography, Thriller/Suspense, eBooks, Self-help, Writing, promotion & publishing, Inspirational/Motivational, History/Political, Adventure, Horror
Comments: I am the owner of Romance At Its Best. We

welcome all authors, new or established. We are a paying site as well. We are for readers, authors, and publishers -- everyone, not just one.

Shari Brennan
Spatium Arena on SimeGen.com
reviews@simegen.com
http://www.simegen.com/reviews/sfreviews/spatiumarena/index.html
Categories: Children's Book, Fiction, General, Literature, Non-Fiction, Sci-Fi/Fantasy, Serials, Young Adult/Children's, Thriller/Suspense, Writing, promotion & publishing, Comics, Adventure
Comments: Contact me via e-mail for submission details.

Brett Axel
various
726 Chestnut St
Utica, NY 13502
WoodstockSlam@hotmail.com
Categories: Art, Audiobooks, Australian Books, Computer/Internet/Technology, Junior College Books, Books From Small Presses, Children's Book, Cookbook, Features, Fiction, Gay/Lesbian Fiction, Gay/Lesbian Non-Fiction, Food, General, Health, How-To, Humanities, Library, Lifestyle, Literature, Marketing, Metaphysical, Mystery, Non-Fiction, Poetry, Pop Culture, Reference, Sci-Fi/Fantasy, Serials, Sociology, Travel/Hospitality, Video, Women, Young Adult/Children's, Psychology/Mental Health, Biography, Parenting, Thriller/Suspense, Theater, Politics, Film History, African-American Fiction and Nonfiction , Financial, Self-help, Writing, promotion & publishing, Comics, Gardening, Science, Education, Scholarly, History/Political, Adventure, Nature, Horror, Photography
Comments: Prefers edgy, daring over mainstream, bland. Only reviews books he likes.

Printing Glossary

Imagesetting

Imagesetting is the new word for phototypesetting. Today's phototypesetting equipment does far more than just set type: it sets images and graphics, too. Originally manufacturers modified existing phototypesetting machines to support *PostScript*, the desktop standard for describing digital page layouts. Today most imagesetters were designed from the ground up to be used in digital pre-press and as such, are capable of reproducing color photographs and graphics at extremely high levels of quality and detail. In a sense an imagesetter is a giant laser printer, but with much higher quality potential. Typical imagesetters produce between 2000 and 5000 dots per inch (versus 600 for business-class lasers). Imagesetters also output directly to film, which is more stable than paper, and at much larger sizes: some imagesetters can output 20"x24" or larger!

PMS

PMS stands for the Pantone Matching System. It's an international system of standard printing ink colors. A unique number identifies each color. (For instance, PMS485 is a bright red.) When you request a particular color to be used in your project we mix it up custom for you (unless we already have that color mixed). Ideally colors should look the same whether printed in Buffalo or Tokyo, but in practice color is extremely subjective and many factors affect how a color prints (such as weather, the paper, etc.).

PMS colors followed by a U or a C (as in PMS485U), stands for Uncoated and Coated, respectively. The ink colors are identical--the only difference is the kind of paper. Colors printed on uncoated paper aren't nearly as bright and vibrant as on coated stock, so make sure you examine the color in the proper guide before making your color decision.

There are thousands of colors available in the Pantone Matching System, including many specialty inks, such as pastels and metalics.

Trapping

Trapping is a general term for compensating for press misregistration by adjusting the artwork of a publication. Every printing press is slightly inaccurate: the paper stretches, curls, and turns, and is impossible to get it perfect. With modern printing equipment the amount of imperfection is minute, however. The only time you would notice misregistration is when there is a visible gap between two overlapping colors and the paper shows through. To compensate for this, the artwork is modified so that the lighter color is *spread*, or made slightly larger, so it actually touches the other color. If this is done properly the press can be slightly off and you will not see an unsightly gap.

Index

About the Author

Alton Pryor has been a writer for magazines, newspapers, and wire services. He worked for United Press International in their Sacramento Bureau, handling both printed press as well as radio news.

He then journeyed to Salinas, where he worked for the Salinas Californian daily newspaper for five years.

In 1963, he joined California Farmer magazine where he worked as a field editor for 27 years. When that magazine was sold, the new owners forced him into retirement, which did not suit him at all.

He then turned to writing books. Alton Pryor is the author of eight books (see page 6). He is a graduate of California State Polytechnic University, San Luis Obispo, where he earned a Bachelor of Science degree in journalism.

Stagecoach Publishing
5360 Campcreek Loop
Roseville, CA. 95747
(916) 771-8166
stagecoachpublishing@surewest.net
www.stagecoachpublishing.com

(The author entertains speaking requests)

____copies "Publish It Yourself" $9.95
____copies "Little Known Tales in California History"
$11.95
____copies "Classic Tales in California History" $11.95
____copies "California's Hidden Gold" $11.95
____copies "Outlaws and Gunslingers" $9.95
____copies "Those Wild and Lusty Gold Camps" $9.95
____copies "Historic California" $9.95
____copies "Jonathan's Red Apple Tree" $3.95

    Name:_____
    Address:_____
    City:_____State:_____Zip:_____
    Telephone: (____)_____
    Shipping and handling: $3.00 for first book, and $1.00 each
    additional book.

Name:_____

Address:_____

_____

Phone: (____) _____